BREAKING THROUGH

Engendering Monitoring and Evaluation in Adult Education

BREAKING THROUGH
Engendering Monitoring and Evaluation in Adult Education

Edited by Carolyn Medel-Añonuevo

 **UNESCO Institute for Education**

* The UNESCO Institute for Education, Hamburg, is a legally independent entity. While the Institute's programmes are established along the lines laid down by the General Conference of UNESCO, the publications of the Institute are issued under its sole responsibility; UNESCO is not responsible for their contents.

The points of view, selection of facts, and opinions expressed are those of the authors and do not necessarily coincide with official positions of the UNESCO Institute of Education, Hamburg.

The designations employed and the presentation of the material in this publication do not imply the expression of any opinion whatsoever on the part of the UNESCO Secretariat concerning the legal status of any country or territory, or its authorities, or concerning the delimitations of the frontiers of any country or territory.

© UNESCO Institute for Education, 1999
Feldbrunnenstr. 58
20148 Hamburg
Germany

ISBN 92 820 1096-1

Printed by
Art Angel Printshop
67 P. Burgos St., Proj. 4
Quezon City, Philippines

ACKNOWLEDGEMENTS

"Breaking Through: Engendering Monitoring and Evaluation in Adult Education" *is the result of the five-day seminar-workshop* "Monitoring and Evaluation from a Gender Perspective" *held at INNOTECH in the Philippines, March 1999.*

Seminar-workshop participants **Margaret Chung, Zenaida Domingo, Celita Eccher, Josefa Francisco, Beata Fiszer, Salma Ismail, Berewa Jommo, Lakshmi Krisnamurthy, Myrna Lim, Sara Longwe, Maureen Pagaduan, Ehsanur Rahman, Roselle Leah Rivera, Sylvia Saca, Meta Amelia Santos, Sofia Valdivielso,** *and* **Fady Yarak** *engaged each other critically and with great curiosity about the monitoring of adult education programmes and projects.*

The staff of INNOTECH not only facilitated our stay in the Philippines but also created a conducive atmosphere for mutual learning. Colleagues at UIE from the Administrative Section, **Klaus Peter Humme, Christian Nowara, Christian Peetz,** *and* **Louise Silz** *lent their support to expedite transactions with the participants and our funders.*

The financial support of the Norwegian government made this meeting and publication possible. The UNESCO Paris Division of Basic Education through **Adama Ouane** *and* **Suzanne Schnuttgen** *supported the participation of one of the women.*

Finally, our warm thanks to **Victoria Tinio** *and* **Patricia Arinto** *for their editorial assistance, to* **Joanne de Leon** *for the cover design of this book, to* **Christian Maramara** *for the layout, and to* **Peter Nelke** *for his technical assistance.*

Carolyn Medel-Anonuevo
Senior Research Specialist on Women's Education

TABLE OF CONTENTS

v ACKNOWLEDGEMENTS

1 INTRODUCTION

5 SARA HLUPEKILE LONGWE
MONITORING AND EVALUATING WOMEN'S EDUCATIONAL PROGRAMMES: CONCEPTS AND METHODOLOGICAL ISSUES

31 PART 1
PRACTICES IN MONITORING AND EVALUATING LITERACY

33 SOFIA VALDIVIELSO GÓMEZ
WOMEN'S PARTICIPATION IN ADULT EDUCATION: THE IALS DATA

43 EHSANUR RAHMAN
MONITORING PARTICIPATION IN LITERACY AND CONTINUING EDUCATION: THE DHAKA AHSANIA MISSION EXPERIENCE

57 FADY YARAK
THE RENÉ MOAWAD FOUNDATION EXPERIENCE IN LEBANON

67 MYRNA LIM
THE WOMEN IN ENTERPRISE DEVELOPMENT (WED) PROJECT: MONITORING AND EVALUATION PRACTICES

83 PART 2
GOING BEYOND QUANTITATIVE MEASURES

85 SALMA ISMAIL
AN EVALUATION OF THE VICTORIA MXENGE HOUSING
DEVELOPMENT ASSOCIATION FROM A GENDER PERSPECTIVE

105 LAKSHMI KRISHNAMURTY
THE MAHILA SAMAKHYA EXPERIENCE

127 BEATA FISZER
EVALUATION IN FEMINIST PROJECTS

135 PART 3
MONITORING INTERNATIONAL COMMITMENTS

137 BEREWA JOMMO
EVALUATING NGO WORK IN EDUCATION FOR ALL
FROM A GENDER PERSPECTIVE

141 CELITA ECCHER
WOMEN PARTICIPATION:
BRIDGING THE GAP

151 MARGARET CHUNG
MONITORING EDUCATION PROGRAMMES
IN PACIFIC ISLAND COUNTRIES

157 JOSEFA FRANCISCO
THE DAWN REVIEW OF THE ICPD IMPLEMENTATION
IN THE SOUTH: SUBSTANTIVE AND METHODOLOGICAL
ASPECTS OF MONITORING

163 APPENDIX

INTRODUCTION

Adult education, gender, and monitoring and evaluation are three separate areas that have undergone redefinition and reconceptualisation in the last ten years. Adult education, which is commonly associated with literacy, basic education, and vocational and technical education, now encompasses, among other things, health education, leadership training, and conflict resolution seminars offered by diverse providers, from the state, the corporate world, academe, and NGOs to people's organisations. Gender, a seemingly neutral concept which refers to the social construction of the sexes, is now a critical topic in development discourses where gender analyses, gender trainings, and gender mainstreaming are considered necessary inputs, processes and outputs for societal transformation. Meanwhile the gurus of quantitative monitoring and evaluation are witnessing a decline in their popularity, as organisations and individuals acknowledge that using both quantitative and qualitative methods render a more nuanced picture of reality. One of the consequences of these changes is the rapid growth and innovation in these different areas.

The UIE-organized international seminar on "Monitoring and Evaluation of Adult Education from a Gender Perspective" held in March 1999 was therefore quite ambitious, as it sought to bring all these three elements together. Finding the participants for this seminar was the first challenge. Very few people would dare claim that their practices in fact involve these three. Yet the seminar was able to bring together women and men from diverse spaces such as the UN and multilateral agencies, governments, NGOs, women's organisations, feminist groups, and universities. And at the end of the day, we were able to agree on some premises.

As gender is one of the more fashionable development concepts, it has been used quite loosely in different circles, blunting its potentialities in the process. The most common example is how gender is used as a synonym for women. When one mentions programs from a gender perspective, the first association is with women's programs. It is easy to say that the substitution of women with gender is part of keeping up with trends. Yet there is a need to examine the schools of thought and political forces that use the concept of gender in order for us to differentiate between those with instrumentalist designs and those who are genuinely motivated to develop this concept as a means to transform societies, communities, relationships, and individuals. Many feminists argue that a critical component of the transformatory discourse is its treatment of gender within a power relations framework.

The Fifth International Conference on Adult Education or CONFINTEA V was an important moment that has helped in expanding the definition of adult education. Yet sweeping generalisations about the explosion of the field of adult education hide the other side of the reality, that of the exclusionary character of many adult education activities. On one hand, there is indeed a growth in the number as well as the content areas of adult education. The increase in provision and diversity is, however, also matched by the increasing number of women and men who have no access to even the most basic education. The gap between those who have access, and whose positions in society are furthered reinforced by such access, and those who have no access, and who remain marginal in society also partly because they have no access, is growing. While corporations invest a lot of funds on their already highly educated managers and staff, many governments cannot even allocate one percent of their budget to adult basic education. The content and pedagogy of educational opportunities also vary across and within countries. It is therefore important that discussions on strategies for strengthening adult education take these into account.

A mapping of the presence, lack or complete absence of policies on adult education is required at this time. For while there is increasing recognition of the importance of adult education in some countries, adult education still needs to be legitimised as part of the education sector in many others. An analysis of how adult education activities in different parts of the world are organised and financed needs to be carried out. Finally, the question of what women and men do with their educational opportunities also needs to be answered. In sum, we are saying that even as the sector is growing, there is still a lot of information lacking.

This is where monitoring and evaluation could be most valuable. Throughout the seminar, we were constantly faced with a set of questions. Why are we monitoring and evaluating? Who should be doing this? How should monitoring and evaluation be carried out? Different presentations had different answers but it was evident that there was growing concern for more participation of the learners in the process. The combined use of quantitative and qualitative measures, as well as of different methods—from self-assessment to group discussions, indicate the growing appreciation for triangulation. This has led to the problematising of the kind of indicators that have to be developed. Indeed, learning is a complex process that cannot be simply measured in terms of months completed or grades earned. The end goal of empowerment of women and of transformed societies, communities and relationships have cognitive, attitudinal and behavioral components that are not easy to measure or study. The process of clarifying, operationalising and implementing such indicators remains a crucial area of work in monitoring and evaluation, and is in fact a key element in engendering monitoring and evaluation.

Once we had shared experiences reflecting the growth and diversity of these areas, the next step was to reflect on how these areas are in fact related, and how critical these interconnections are to our work. **Breaking Through: Engendering Monitoring and Evaluation in Adult Education** presents the rich discussion of these inter-relationships during the seminar. As women and men of different backgrounds came together, simply listening and trying to level-off was the first order of the day. Some participants were anxious to have a conceptual framework spelled out right at the beginning of the seminar. Others agreed, however, that while framework-setting was important, the state of the art of these three areas warranted a more inductive approach. Throughout the five-day seminar, as we continued to clarify our concepts and practices, discussions shifted from the abstract to the practical to the political. It is hoped that this publication has been able to capture the essence of this process.

The first article, written by Sara Longwe, presents a conceptual framework for monitoring and evaluation. Although this framework set the tone of the discussion, it was not meant to be definitive nor was it used by all the participants. The rest of the publication is divided into three main parts. The first part looks at the range of monitoring and evaluation practices in literacy while the second presents examples of practices that went beyond literacy and discusses various qualitative measures. The last section presents the latest mode of monitoring, that of looking at governments' international commitments and examining to what extent they are able to fulfill such promises. A summary of the indicators of empowerment developed by CENZONTLE as well as the output of the group work of the participants during the seminar are found in the Appendix.

The seminar is indeed only a starting point, but we feel that we are breaking through. The experiences and analyses of the presenters have been most critical in this. Sara Longwe, who is from Zambia, is Chairperson of FEMNET, the African Women's Development and Communication Network, and is also a consultant on women's research and gender training. For the first section on monitoring and evaluating literacy practices, we have contributions from Sofia Valdivielso Gómez, a literacy teacher and researcher working with the government of Spain in the Gran Canary Islands; Ehsanur Rahman, Director of the Programmes Division of the Dhaka Ahsania Mission, an NGO in Bangladesh; Fady Yarak, Development and Programme Manager of the René Moawad Foundation, an NGO in Lebanon; and Myrna Lim, Executive Director of the Notre Dame Foundation for Charitable Activities, an organization based in Southern Philippines.

Contributions for the second section, "Going Beyond Quantitative Measures," are from Salma Ismail, who teaches at the Department of Adult Education and Extra-Mural Studies, University of Cape Town; Beata Fiszer, one of the founders of the PSF Women's Center in Warsaw, Poland; and Lakshmi Krishnamurty, an educator from Alarippu, an NGO working in New Delhi, India.

For the final section, we have contributions from Berewa Jommo of the African Community Education Network, who is also Regional Coordinator of the International Community Education Association in Africa; Margaret Chung, a researcher and consultant on several UN as well as NGO projects; Celita Eccher, Coordinator of the Gender Education Office of the International Council for Adult Education and REPEM, the network of popular educators of women in Latin America and the Carribean; and Josefa Francisco, Southeast Asia Regional Coordinator of DAWN or Developing Alternatives for Women in the New Era.

Monitoring and Evaluating Women's Educational Programmes:
Concepts and Methodological Issues

Sara Hlupekile Longwe

INTRODUCTION

This paper presents some of the basic concepts of monitoring and evaluation that could be considered when monitoring women's adult education programmes. These concepts provide the vocabulary for analysing methodological issues that are likely to arise in monitoring progress towards better education for women.

A women's literacy programme is analysed to illustrate the utilisation of concepts, and also to refer to some of the main methodological issues that need to be recognised and addressed in women's adult education programmes. In examining these concepts and issues, there is also a special interest in their relevance to better methods for monitoring government efforts to implement CONFINTEA V declarations concerned with improving adult education for women. (See Appendix for some proposed indicators.) The paper concludes by raising some of the main methodological issues that were identified during the discussion of concepts and methods.

CONCEPTUAL FRAMEWORK

THE BASIC CONCEPT OF MONITORING AND EVALUATION

Monitoring and evaluation (M&E) refers to the process of assessing progress over time. *Monitoring* refers to the collection of data according to well-specified indicators. *Evaluation* involves the use of this data for the assessment of progress. M&E begins with the identification of a *variable* to be monitored over time, e.g., "level of adult women's literacy" More specifically, we are interested in how this variable changes over time, or progress.

A variable is more precise if it identifies a well-defined *indicator*. An indicator specifies the *unit of measure* of the data to be collected, which may also imply the type of analysis that needs to be done in order to manipulate the raw data collected.

MONITORING OF QUANTITATIVE VARIABLES

Most M&E is based on quantitative measures of progress over time. A quantitative variable should be clear and specific, and not composite. For example, CONFINTEA V Paragraph 25 includes the variable:

> *Degree of advancement with respect to the goal of reducing female illiteracy by the year 2000 to half of the 1990 rate, for a fixed year.*

This is a typical statement of a variable of interest in M&E. The statement includes the *quantity* in which one is interested (female illiteracy), the interest in *progress over time*, and the *criterion* for evaluating the adequacy of progress (the target of halving female illiteracy by the year 2000). The information on quantity and progress are essential to monitoring, which involves the collection of data over time. Criteria should be spelled out before any evaluation of the adequacy of progress revealed by the data can be made.

However, the variable is not well defined unless it specifies the indicator to be used in measuring the variable. If the indicator is not specified, different data will be collected in different countries and the information will not be useful for an inter-country comparison.

The sample variable given above might be measured by the indicator

> *change per year in the percentage of the female adult population that is illiterate*

However, from a gender point of view, there should be interest in the position of women relative to men. In this case, it would be necessary to add another indicator:

> *change per year in the gender gap between the percentage of illiterates in the female and male adult populations.*

The general importance of *gender gap* as an indicator is discussed further in a later section.

Qualitative Monitoring

It is much more difficult to monitor progress in terms of improved quality over time. CONFINTEA V Paragraph 13 suggests the following variable to be monitored:

> *Contents on equity and equality in gender, race, age, and ethnicity relations introduced in the curricula of formal education at all levels*

Measuring progress on this variable would involve a quantitative component variable of progress in introducing curriculum components. But clearly progress also has to do with the *quality* of the new curriculum content.

The above variable is unhelpful to the evaluator seeking indicators of progress. It is composite in that it is concerned with assessing curricula in the area of gender, rate, age and ethnicity. Second, the variable is composite in that it is concerned with both quantity (new curriculum contents) and quality (education for equity and equality within the new contents).

Another interesting aspect of the above variable is that it seems to be largely concerned with *inputs* into the educational system (the curricula), rather than the *outputs* (of educated people). But it may also imply an interest in progress of the curricular process, in terms of learning activities and transactions.

Inputs versus Outputs

In a simple systems analysis, M&E may be focused on any one of the three essential stages in an input-output process:

INPUT ——— PROCESS ——— OUTPUT

In the case of literacy education, the three components will look something like this:

Input	iliterate adults, teachers, curriculum materials
Process	literacy curriculum, as a sequence of learning activities
Output	literate adults

In monitoring the success of such a system, the ideal option is obviously to look at the outputs. Monitoring outputs is the easier and more quantitative form of monitoring.

Here monitoring of outputs might be extended to include the qualitative component of the level of literacy of the output, as well as their numbers. Alternatively, if quality control is considered part of the process (as the final stage of awarding certificates), then output monitoring may then consist only of quantitative monitoring of certificate production.

However, if it is not possible to monitor the output, or if the output results are unsatisfactory, then it becomes necessary to find out what is going on at the preceding stages of input and process. (It hardly needs pointing out that if either the inputs or the process is grossly inappropriate or inadequate, there can be no logical output!)

As process becomes the focus of interest in M&E, then quality is likely to become the focus of evaluation interest. In the example above, process might to some extent be measured in terms of the number of classes, the number of students, the frequency of attendance, and so on. But a large part of the assessment of process must be concerned with quality.

The quality of the process is a key concern in education for women's empowerment. For example, in literacy education for women, a basic question is whether literacy is for the purpose of enabling women to adapt to or be more integrated within the given patriarchal world (i.e., literacy for understanding instruction manuals), or whether it is literacy for conscientisation (i.e., literacy for reinterpreting and problematising the patriarchal world).

MONITORING FOR A SITUATION ANALYSIS

The foregoing discussion draws attention to the question of whether M&E is being done as part of a *situation analysis*, or whether M&E is part of assessing the progress of a *project intervention*.

In a situation analysis, the evaluator merely monitors changes in the overall socio-economic situation. The evaluators are passive observers because they are not involved in trying to change the situation, but are merely recording changes. These changes may be due to natural trends over time, or are the results of developmental interventions by government or other agencies.

In a situation analysis, it is more usual for the evaluators to confine their interest to the outputs, to the exclusion of the inputs, process, or other aspects of the situation that led to the outputs. In other words, the evaluators are concerned with the observable socio-economic status of people, the infrastructural situation, and so on. However, when the analysis of the situation reveals unsatisfactory aspects (i.e., development issues), the evaluators may take an interest in the *underlying causes* that have given rise to these unsatisfactory aspects.

Conceptual Framework for Underlying Causes of a Gender Issue

A situation analysis may use a three-point analysis of each gender issue, whereby the three essential elements of a gender issue are considered: gender gap, gender discrimination, and gender oppression.

The empirical manifestation of the issue is the existence of a gender gap, the immediate underlying cause of which is discriminatory practices. These in turn are maintained by the patriarchal interest in keeping women in a subordinate position. More specifically, we may define a *gender gap* as a measure of gender inequality on any particular socio-economic indicator. It is a difference in any aspect between the socio-economic status of women and that of men. The gap arises not from a biological difference between women and men, but from their different gender roles and social locations. At the public level a gender gap is often observable and even measurable, and may be part of well-known statistics.

In a literacy situation, there is gender gap of 30 percent if 70 percent of males are literate while only 40 percent women are literate. A very large number of gender statistics can easily be put into the form of a gender gap. This standardised indicator makes for easy comparison between one indicator and another, and for making inter-country comparisons.

Gender gaps do not arise by accident; they are caused by the different treatment given to girls and women, relative to the treatment given to boys and men. This is what is meant by *gender discrimination*, here defined as the different treatment given to one gender in comparison with the other. Gender discrimination could be a single instance, as when an employer selects a man for employment when a woman has the better qualifications. However, a national pattern of gender gaps reveals something much more than isolated instances of discrimination. Gender gaps at the national level are due to systemic gender discrimination, or discrimination that is part of most aspects of the social system (legal, administrative, and traditional).

The gender gap in literacy, for example, may have been caused by various discriminatory practices, such as the parental decision to send their sons to school and to keep their daughters at home, discrimination in the schools' treatment of girls, patriarchal messages in curriculum materials, and lack of literature available for women.

Discriminatory treatment of women does not arise by cultural accident, but is itself a means for the oppression of women. Discriminatory practice is the means by which men maintain their domination over women. The male monopoly of decision-making, even at the household level, is used to maintain male privilege and to preserve male leisure. While the male may claim that he is making decisions for the general benefit of the household, the actual effect is usually that he allocates to himself the larger part of the resources, and to his wife the larger part of the labour which produces these resources.

Therefore, underlying the systemic discrimination against women is the maintenance of patriarchal power: male domination of power within the home and government for the purpose of maintaining male privilege.

In analysing patriarchal oppression, it is useful to distinguish between *control*, *interest* and *belief*. The higher level of literacy of a husband facilitates his control over his less literate wife. He has an interest in his wife being less knowledgeable than himself, since this difference in education is used to legitimise his monopoly of decision-making in the household. Denying women education is legitimised by traditional beliefs that women do not need education (because of the traditional belief in their domestic role), and by the belief that women are less capable of benefiting from education (because of the sexist belief in women's biological inferiority).

In the monitoring and evaluation of programmes for women's empowerment, several methodological issues arise from the type of analysis described above. The first is that most analysis of women's situation is confined to the "gender-gap" level. This kind of information is more easily obtainable and quantifiable, and therefore useful for measuring trends over time and making inter-country comparisons. In comparison, the qualitative information on discriminatory practices is much more difficult to collect and systematise, and does not provide easy measures of progress.

However, gender gaps are merely the surface manifestation of deeper problems. There is a need to monitor whether progress is being made in addressing underlying causes. When progress is not being made in closing gender gaps, it is important to look into the causes of lack of progress. Are programme interventions aiming for superficial and cosmetic changes in the statistics, without addressing underlying causes?

For example, there might be increasing numbers of women graduating from literacy classes, without this altering actual levels of literacy (because the literacy skills they acquire are of little practical use, and "fall away" with time). Alternatively, increasing levels of literacy may not have the intended purpose of contributing to increased empowerment of women.

Even at the level of collecting data on gender gaps, serious methodological issues may arise. In Third World countries, data on the overall socio-economic situation is difficult to find. It is probably not collected by public institutions or by any centralised Office of Statistics. The collected data is often not disaggregated by gender. Thus, monitors of women's progress may find that they need a lot of time for re-analysing and disaggregating existing data, or otherwise mounting a research effort to collect raw data. From this point of view, it can be very unhelpful for CONFINTEA V to write a set of "ideal" variables and indicators for monitoring progress in women's adult education.

The problem of monitoring also has to be approached from the opposite direction, i.e., finding out which categories of information are commonly available from public institutions, and what additional information the monitors can realistically be expected to collect. Monitoring can then be based on a realistic set of variables and indicators. Another consideration is that a patriarchal government is naturally reluctant to collect information that graphically reveals its own discrimination against women.

MONITORING PROGRAMME INTERVENTION

Where educational outputs are the result of a national programme of educational reform, or new educational provision, then monitoring progress may well involve more than a realisation of outputs.

In evaluating the success of a developmental intervention, it is useful to distinguish between five different types of evaluation questions: appropriateness, adequacy, progress, effectiveness, and efficiency.

APPROPRIATENESS

This is the most basic question that can be asked about any aspect of a development programme. This has to do with rightness or relevance. For example, we might ask whether literacy materials are appropriate for the target group, or for women members of the target group, or whether they are appropriate as a means to increased empowerment for women.

ADEQUACY

Once we have satisfied ourselves about questions of appropriateness, we are then in a position to ask whether a particular aspect of a project is adequate, in terms of whether it is sufficient or whether enough is being done. For example, we might look at whether there is a sufficient number of literacy materials, or whether the materials go far enough in developing literacy skills.

Progress

The question of progress is the question of whether the project is being implemented in a timely manner, in order to meet targets and complete the programme on schedule. This is partly a matter of whether there is adequate progress over time, measured mainly in terms of the provision of programme inputs over time, as well as programme process (implementation activities) over time. In the later stages, M&E may look at outputs, or effectiveness over time. Therefore, the question of progress is intermediate between adequacy and effectiveness, with the emphasis on progress over time in programme implementation.

Effectiveness

This is the question of whether the programme is effective in achieving the intended results. At its most basic level, the question has to do with whether the programme is producing the intended outcomes and benefits, as expressed in the programme objectives. In literacy education for women, effectiveness would be measured in terms of such indicators as coverage of the target group, increase in percentage of women who are literate, and narrowing the gender gap in illiteracy.

Efficiency

This question goes one stage further than the question of effectiveness, to ask the question of whether programme outcomes were obtained with a minimum use of resources. At its most basic level, lack of efficiency is revealed by waste and use of unproductive methods.

The foregoing definitions reveal the inter-connections between the five types of question, as a logical sequence. In monitoring and evaluating a particular programme activity, the question of appropriateness needs to be settled before questions of adequacy are asked. There is no point in asking whether progress is being made in implementing an activity if this activity is not appropriate as a means for pursuing project objectives. For example, it is not useful to measure the effectiveness of a literacy programme purely in terms of the number trained, without first assessing the appropriateness of the literacy curriculum. Similarly, schooling cannot be equated with education unless a prior assessment has been made of the educational content of the school curriculum. Such considerations are crucial in education for women's empowerment, as schooling may have the effect of making women more submissive and subordinate.

Monitoring in the Context of Overall Programme Evaluation

If programme activities are not appropriate for achieving programme objectives, then one cannot expect the intended outcomes. Therefore, it is important that monitoring and evaluation of outcomes should be seen in the general context of the appropriateness of the overall programme.

Table 1 shows an example of a national programme for women's literacy education. The column on "Description of the Programme" shows the typical form of a women's literacy programme in Southern Africa, together with the usual (implicit) claims that improved literacy will "automatically" lead to increased productivity and empowerment for women. However, the two columns on "Evaluation Questions to be Asked" and "Likely Answers to the Questions" raise serious doubts about whether such a programme really has anything to do with women's empowerment. In fact, some of the answers to the questions suggest that the classes may be disempowering, and contribute only to the increased subordination of women.

This table is presented to illustrate the inadequacy of monitoring the success of a programme purely in terms of a quantitative measure of outcomes (in this case the numbers of women who become literate, or the increase in the percentage of women in the literate population). There is a need to consider the adequacy of the analysis of the original problem, and the appropriateness of the implementation strategy, before the monitoring of outcomes can be taken at face value. In addition, there is a need for M&E to include an interest in the *quality* of the activities, which contributed to the outcomes, in terms of women's participation, and the relevance of women's learning activities as a contribution to their increased productivity and empowerment.

These considerations lead us to the next part of this paper: the need for more emphasis on process monitoring; and the prospects for qualitative as well as quantitative monitoring. In the area of qualitative monitoring, the fundamental question is whether education is for subordination, or empowerment. Are women being taught to know their place, or are they learning to escape from it?

Table 1 starts on the next page.

STAGE OF PROGRAMME	DESCRIPTION OF PROGRAMME
SITUATION ANALYSIS	Of the general adult population, 30 percent are illiterate: 45 percent amongst the females and 15 percent amongst men. This is widely considered to be the main reason for women's lack of occupation of decision-making positions in the community, and for women's low productivity.cc
POLICY ENVIRONMENT	There is a national policy principle of equality of opportunity for both females and males in access to all educational services.
PROBLEM IDENTIFICATION	• The large proportion of women among the illiterate • Women's low productivity and poor representation in decision-making positions due to their low levels of literacy
PROGRAMME OBJECTIVES	• To increase the literacy rate among adult women from 15 percent to 45 percent over a five year period • To empower women by giving them literacy skills
IMPLEMENTATION STRATEGY	To organise weekly literacy classes for adult women of each community, and to use existing literacy materials
PROJECT ACTIVITIES	• To train 1,000 literacy teachers for a two-year literacy campaign • To form 1,000 literacy classes throughout the country • To monitor progress in terms of teachers trained, enrolments, and numbers of graduates
PROJECT OUTCOMES	To make 60,000 women literate over the two-year programme period

QUESTIONS WHEN LOOKING AT A DEVELOPMENT PROGRAM

EVALUATION QUESTIONS TO BE ASKED	LIKELY ANSWERS TO THE QUESTIONS
• Is lack of literacy really a main reason for women's lack of occupation of decision-making positions? • Is there discrimination against women in access to schooling and to literacy education? • In what ways would women's increased literacy lead to increased empowerment?	• Women's lack of occupation of decision-making positions is largely due to gender discrimination in access to these positions. • Women's burden of household labour is a main factor that makes it difficult for them to find the time to attend literacy classes.
• Does the policy environment allow for the gender problems to be addressed? • Is there policy support for affirmative action to overcome gender discrimination and enable all-women literacy classes?	• Gender discrimination is well entrenched at the traditional and administrative levels, despite national policy statements • Literacy classes concerned with women's empowerment rather than merely technical literacy skills are likely to be resisted by the patriarchal establishment.
• Is improved literacy likely to improve women's productivity? Will it lead to increased self-reliance? Will it lead to women's increased empowerment? • In what ways can literacy improve women's ability to recognise and address the gender issues that stand in the way of increased productivity?	• Many illiterate women were taught to read and write at school, but their literacy has since fallen away from them. Literacy seems to have little functional purpose, and there is little literature available in the village. • Women's literacy needs to be clearly related to the process of increased self-reliance and empowerment.
• Do the project objectives also address the underlying gender issues that stand in the way of women's literacy, and retention of literacy? • How is the objective of literacy related to the objective of empowerment?	The objectives do not mention any gender issues, or gender discrimination standing in the way of literacy, or using literacy skills to overcome discrimination and increase women's control over resources.
• Does the system of literacy classes take account of women's difficulty in finding the time to attend such classes, given their heavy burden of labour? How will the programme overcome the problem of husbands not giving their wives permission to attend classes? Are literacy materials appropriate? • Are existing literacy materials appropriate for women, and for education for women's increased self-reliance and empowerment?	• Women are not likely to find time for the classes. Instead, literacy education could have been incorporated within existing women's group activities. • If women have to ask permission, husbands are likely to refuse. • Existing literacy materials are based on primary school books, and therefore treat the readers as if they are small children.
• Are the teachers women or men? What do the teachers know about the process of women's empowerment, and identifying gender issues? • How does a class use improved literacy to discuss issues of women's increased empowerment? • What influence or control do the members of the class have over the curriculum content and methods?	• The literacy classes are a top-down imposition of pre-prepared materials that are more suitable for children. • Both the content and form of the curriculum are insulting and disempowering to the adult women who attend.
What is the expected outcome in terms of women's increased empowerment?	Given the original project objectives, there is a need to assess outcomes in terms of whether graduates from the scheme subsequently improve their productivity, income-earning ability, and occupation of decision-making positions.

Different Types of Monitoring

The following are the different types of monitoring:

- *Input monitoring* means keeping a record of whether the promised inputs have been provided in a timely fashion, and whether the programme is on schedule in requesting and utilising these inputs. Here an example of an indicator would be the yearly government budget for women's adult education as a percentage of the budget for all government provision on adult education and as a percentage of the total government budget. Another input indicator would be the numbers of curriculum booklets produced for a national literacy programme.

- *Activity monitoring* involves monitoring whether activities are taking place as planned. For instance, an indicator might be concerned with the yearly number of literacy classes, enrolment and percentage of women enroled. Less quantitative but often interesting is looking at progress along a predetermined sequence of *milestones or benchmarks*, e.g., government progress in 1) drawing up a policy on women's adult education, 2) drawing up a strategic plan, 3) training teachers, 4) developing curriculum materials, etc.

- *Process monitoring*, a fundamental aspect of activity monitoring, involves monitoring the appropriateness of the implementation methods being used, in terms of whether they match the specified implementation strategy. Because of our interest in the process of women's empowerment, we should clearly identify the indicators of whether the programme is enabling and promoting this process as a central method of project implementation.

Indicators in this area of monitoring are mainly qualitative, and may involve some innovation. Process evaluation is an underdeveloped area of M&E, which has traditionally been overly focused on outcomes and impact to the relative exclusion of the process by which outcomes are achieved. Monitoring the process of women's empowerment requires the identification of indicators based on the *process of women's empowerment*. Sections 2.10 and 2.11 look further at this problem area.

Output monitoring involves monitoring progress in direct programme outputs. In an adult literacy programme, the initial and direct outputs might be trained teachers and curriculum materials. There is a distinction between the direct output and its subsequent *effects* in terms of the *outcome* and *impact*, which are considered below.

Outcome monitoring means measuring the *results* of programme intervention. In a women's literacy programme, the intended outcome might be defined as the literacy of women who were previously illiterate.

Impact monitoring involves monitoring the after effects or *long-term results* and *unintended effects* of the outputs and outcomes. In an adult literacy programme, it might be intended that women's improved literacy would lead to women's mobilisation and conscientisation for increasing their capacity to recognising and addressing gender issues. But does the programme actually result in this long-term development of women's collective capacity?

A Framework for Understanding Women's Empowerment

In monitoring and evaluating the process of women's empowerment, we are primarily concerned with qualitative aspects of process, rather than quantitative aspects of outcomes. Without an appropriate process, there is no rational prospect of achieving the desired outcomes.

Monitoring and evaluation of women's increased empowerment must be based on evaluation criteria that are rooted in an understanding of the process of women's empowerment. One way of analysing this process is in terms of the Women's Empowerment Framework, which identifies five levels of (inter-related) progress towards women's empowerment:

Women's Empowerment Framework[2]

Levels of Equality	Increased Equality	Increased Empowerment
Control		
Mobilisation		
Conscientisation		
Access		
Welfare		

- Welfare refers to the level of the material welfare and socio-economic status of females, relative to males. Here we describe gender gaps in terms of whether women are mere statistics, or passive recipients of welfare benefits, rather than individuals capable of changing their lives. The welfare level of monitoring women's literacy would be concerned with monitoring women's current level of literacy, e.g., the percentage of literates in the population of adult women. Action to improve literacy will entail access to literacy education, which involves addressing inequality at the next level.

- *Access.* The gender gap at the welfare level arises directly from inequality of access to resources. Women's lower levels of productivity arise, in the first instance, from their restricted access to the resources for development and production available in the society, namely, land, credit, labour and services. Gender gaps in literacy arise from women's relative lack of access to primary schooling, and perhaps also to lack of access to adult literacy classes. Thus, it would be interesting to monitor progress in women's increased access to primary schooling and literacy education. Output indicators might be concerned with gender gaps in school enrolments and in literacy classes.

> Within this framework, "equality of access to resources" is seen as a step to women's advancement. But the next level of the framework considers women's present lack of access to resources as a result of systems of gender discrimination. When women try to overcome the obstacles to access, they have to confront the systemic discrimination that can be addressed only through the empowerment process of conscientisation.

- *Conscientisation.* Here the gender gap is not empirical, but is a belief-gap, i.e., the belief that women's lower socio-economic position, and the traditional gender division of labour, is part of the natural order or is "God given". This conception of the gender gap is usually reflected and conveyed in everyday messages in the mass media and school textbooks. Empowerment means sensitisation to such beliefs and their rejection. It means recognising that women's subordination is not part of the natural order of things, but is imposed by a system of discrimination which is socially constructed and which can be altered.

> This level of equality involves the individual's conceptualisation of the development process in terms of structural inequality: the realisation that women's problems do not derive so much from their own personal inadequacies as from a social system of

institutionalised discrimination against women and girls. This involves the ability to critically analyse society and recognise as discriminatory those practices which were previously accepted as "normal" or part of the permanent "given world" which cannot be changed. This involves understanding the distinction between sex roles and gender roles, in particular that the latter are sociocultural and can be changed.

Above all, it means women's rejection of the "given" patriarchal perception of women and of their "proper" role and place. Instead of accepting the male perception of women, women collectively come to a different understanding of their role, their worth, and their rights. Women no longer seek success on men's terms, or seek a place as an "honorary male" within a male dominated world. Instead, they seek to enlarge female perception, find their authentic female voice, and pursue female interests. If literacy can facilitate this process, then it contributes to women's empowerment.

It would be interesting to monitor the discriminatory rules and practices standing in the way of women's access to school and literacy education. From the point of view of literacy education itself, there should be an interest in whether this education contributes to the process of women's conscientisation, as a means to collective mobilisation and action on the various forms of gender discrimination that diminish their access to resources and limit their control over their own lives.

- *Mobilisation*. The individual woman in the home is not likely to make much progress in challenging traditional assumptions. It is when women get together that they are able to collectively discuss gender issues. They need to analyse the burden of labour placed upon them as women, the discriminatory practices that put them at a disadvantage, and the male domination of decision-making that stands in the way of doing things differently.

  Mobilisation is therefore the fourth and crucial stage of empowerment. It enables the collective analysis of gender issues and the collective commitment to action. Mobilisation is also largely concerned with achieving participation in decision-making.

In monitoring and evaluating a literacy programme, the qualitative question is whether the programme is contributing to the process of women's empowerment by providing part of the means by which women can meet together to recognise and analyse gender issues, and agree on collective action to address specific gender issues. The question, therefore, is whether literacy education contributes to this mobilisation process, and whether improved literacy provides the means to improved discussion and mobilisation (e.g., through flip-chart discussions, records of meetings, notices of meetings, communications with other groups, etc.).

- *Control.* At the level of control, the gender gap is manifested as the unequal power relations between women and men. For instance, within the household, a husband's control over his wife's labour, and of the resulting cash income, means that a wife's increased productivity may not result in increased welfare for herself and her children. In this instance, the gender gap is the gap between effort and reward: the wife makes the effort but the husband collects the reward.

  Increased participation of women at the decision-making level will lead to increased development and empowerment of women when this participation is used to achieve increased control over the factors of production, to ensure women's equal access to resources and the distribution of benefits. *Equality of control* means a balance of power between women and men, so that neither is in a position of dominance. It means that women have power alongside men to influence their destiny and that of their society.

  It is equality of control that enables women to gain improved access to resources, and therefore enables improved welfare for themselves and their children. We should not think of welfare goals as being lesser or lower level goals; rather, we view equality of control as a necessary prerequisite if we are to make progress toward gender equality in welfare provision.

  In the process type of M&E of literacy education, there might be an interest in the extent to which women increasingly control the activities and interests of literacy classes in order to build vocabulary and literacy around the discussion of gender issues which interest them. From an outcome point of view, there might be an interest in monitoring whether women's literacy classes subsequently enable women to take more control over their own lives in such matters as control over resources like land or household income.

AN EXAMPLE OF MONITORING WOMEN'S EMPOWERMENT

Table 2 takes the example of a national programme for women's literacy education. The very bare description given in the chart may well suggest a rather inadequate programme. However, the purpose here is merely to show how the literacy programme may develop an interest in the empowerment process, and then to speculate on some of the evaluation questions and methods that are necessary for the proper monitoring and evaluation of the programme.

The Women's Empowerment Framework discussed above provides the evaluation criteria for monitoring the extent to which the project is enabling the process of empowerment.

The examples in Table 2 show that the welfare and access aspects of empowerment are more easily monitored by quantitative indicators. Conversely, those aspects of the project which are more central and intrinsic to the empowerment process are more difficult to monitor and call for a qualitative assessment of the worthwhileness of progress.

Table 2 also reveals that, although process evaluation may not be particularly concerned with qualitative outcomes, it can nonetheless be very systematic and explicit. Assessment may be based on qualitative judgement rather than quantitative measure, but such judgement can be made on the basis of explicit evidence and explicit evaluation criteria. In this way, evaluation findings have validity and reliability, are accessible to outside readers, and are useful for inter-country comparisons.

Table 2 starts on the next page.

EMPOWERMENT LEVEL	PROGRAMME ACTIVITY	ASPECT OF EMPOWERMENT
WELFARE	Increase the proportion of literates among adult women in the community	Literate women are assumed to be less dependent, more self-reliant
ACCESS	Provision of literacy classes for women, flexible hours, overcoming discrimination in access	Benefits of literacy depend on women's access to literacy classes
CONSCIENTISATION	Use of literacy classes to discuss gender relations and gender discrimination; literacy as a means for the discussion of dissatisfaction.	Women's realisation of human rights and dignity, and injustice of discrimination, and that the situation does not have to be accepted
MOBILISATION	Construct literacy classes as a means towards women's increased understanding and action on gender issues.	Women use the group discussions to collective effort to analyse their situation and take action to improve their situation.
CONTROL	Classes designed for participation in curriculum topics, and use of literacy for pursuit of women's interests. Decision on content of curriculum discussion and on action to address gender issues affecting the community.	Action to take control on (one or more) gender issues that improve women's control over decision-making, e.g., increase wives control over literacy curriculum, or over household income.

EVALUATION QUESTION	EVALUATION VARIABLE	EVALUATION METHOD
Has the programme reached its target in increasing the proportion of literates among women, and in reducing gender gaps in literacy?	Percentage of literates among women; gender gaps in literacy	Pre-programme and post-programme literacy tests on (a sample of) the target group; proportion of the target group certified as literate.
• What is the progress in women's enrolment in literacy classes? • What are the barriers to women's access to literacy classes?	• Women's enrolment over time, gender gaps in enrolment. • Progress is lessening obstacles to women's participation.	• Collection of data on frequency of classes and gender disaggregated figures on enrolments. • Progress on removing. Milestones in progress toward eliminating discriminatory obstacles to class attendance.
• Does the curriculum enable and facilitate the discussion of local gender issues? • Have women increased their sense of injustice, and their willingness to take action?	Frequency of literacy classes making suggestions for action to challenge the current traditions that discriminate against women.	Monitor classes and feedback from teachers for frequency of radical and non-conformist statements on gender issues
Are class members taking follow-up action outside the classroom? Has progress on addressing a gender issue become a focus of classroom discussion?	Formation of committees and action groups. Frequency of decisions to take collective action. Production of written communications for facilitate group cohesion and action	Feedback from teachers, and reports of outcomes from literacy class meetings. Frequency of production of documents to facilitate group understanding and action.
In what ways have women class members increased their control within particular aspects of gender relations outside the classroom?	Women's collective action to increase women's control over decisions within the household; women's occupation of decision-making position within the community; examples of discriminatory practices which have been changed as the result of women's collective action.	Records kept by teachers, key informants in the community: Post-programme interviews with sample of graduates and other key informants.

SOME METHODOLOGICAL ISSUES IN MONITORING WOMEN'S EDUCATION PROGRAMMES

This concluding section looks back at the preceding discussion of concepts and methods to identify and explore the main methodological issues.

SPECIFICITY OF QUANTITATIVE INDICATORS

It is important for the indicators of progress to be very clearly stated. In the case of quantitative indicators, the variable to be measured should include specific and well-defined information on the indicator of progress in terms of the unit of measure and the criteria for acceptable progress.

For example, the variable *women's level of literacy* may be defined in terms of indicators of:

1) The percentage of adult women who are illiterate;
2) The gender gap as the percentage difference between the level of illiteracy of adult women relative to that of adult men.

Criteria for acceptable progress should also be mentioned, e.g., halving the percentage of women who are illiterate during the period 1990-2000.

The stated variable should be explicit and should not be a composite of several variables. The following variable, from CONFINTEA V, Paragraph 12, is *not* a good example:

> *The existence of governmental educational programmes addressed to women at the levels of race, gender, small business owners, and/or community leaders.*

This variable is composite and not explicit. Moreover, it does not seem to call for an indicator to measure progress over time but merely seeks data of the existence of programmes, i.e., information on whether they exist or not. On the face of it, the variable calls for a "yes" or "no" response.

Perhaps what is implied but not stated is the need to measure the progress of such programmes in terms of the numbers of different programmes and the enrolment of women in these programmes, both to be monitored over time.

Specificity of Qualitative Indicators

Much of the discussion in the first half of this paper was concerned with conceptualising the problem of qualitative indicators. It was argued that, in the area of women's education, it is necessary to monitor qualitative indicators for assessing the quality of outputs (and not merely their quantity), and to assess the quality of the process by which the outputs are achieved.

The variable presented in CONFINTEA V Paragraph 13 is *not* very helpful:

> *Contents on equity and equality in gender ... in the curricula of formal education at all levels*

If this is a "yes" or "no" question, it is a trivial quantitative question which is not going to give much information or suggest a means to measure progress. Clearly, there is a need for a better specification of the indicator for measuring the quantity and quality of the gender oriented curriculum materials.

The need for quantification demands a well-defined quantitative indicator. The need for qualitative evaluation demands the specification of the criteria by which the gender orientation of curriculum materials is to be assessed. If the criteria are not specified, then it is likely that different categories of data will be collected by different research teams in different countries. The results may not be of much use for monitoring progress in one country or for making inter-country comparisons.

Collecting the Collectable

The example given in the preceeding section shows how easy it is to write a variable which seems meaningful to the authors but which will subsequently put the monitors in a terrible fix.

The authors of schemes for monitoring and evaluation must do more than dream about all the information that they would ideally like to collect. If the information sought is described in terms of a long list of composite variables, it is very likely that much of this information will not be easily obtainable. Even if they were all available and obtainable, they might well add up to more information than can be collected, analysed, and utilised.

Therefore, the problem of monitoring boils down to the question of selecting the key indicators of progress based on the essential information that is strongly indicative of the general situation, and that is easily collectable in the countries being studied. Where possible, and especially in the area of quantitative monitoring, indicators should be based on data that is already routinely collected by government departments as part of their normal administration and management. To go beyond this category of data is likely to give monitors a task that is enormous, or even impossible.

ACCESS VERSUS EMPOWERMENT

The issues of specificity and collectability arise perhaps more at the level of method rather than methodology. In the remainder of this concluding section, we come to the deeper methodological issues that bear on the assumptions and theory underpinning our methods.

The earlier discussion shows that the quantitative monitoring of outputs is based on assumptions of the appropriateness of the interventions that produce these outputs, as a means to women's advancement and empowerment.

Often, it is assumed that women's increased access to literacy skills, as well as higher forms of education, will automatically lead to their increased self-reliance and empowerment. But this is not always the case. Thus, we should also be monitoring:

- whether the content and method of education provided is appropriate for women's advancement and empowerment; and
- whether programmes have educational outcomes and impact that actually show women's increased empowerment after the educational experience.

SCHOOLING VERSUS EDUCATION

Underlying the use of educational outputs as a means for monitoring progress is the assumption that the process which produced the outputs was really educational according to our understanding of the meaning of "education". However, this assumption is not always valid.

In the case of women's adult education, it might well be asked whether the courses lead to women's increased subordination or to women's empowerment. Insofar as adult education classes reflect and replicate the top-down relationships of the primary classroom, and insofar and they perpetuate and reinforce the traditional pattern of gender relations, then such education is subordinating rather than liberating and empowering.[3]

A recent study of all African countries looks at the correlation between gender gaps in educational levels and gender gaps in parliament. It was found that there is absolutely no correlation between the women's level of schooling in a particular country and their level of representation in parliament.[4] In other words, there were some countries where the women's level of schooling is high but their representation in parliament is low. Similarly, there are some countries where the women's level of schooling is low but their representation in parliament is high. Schooling was not found to be a predictor for women's occupation of decision-making positions. This lack of correlation between women's schooling was also observed in other decision-making positions such as higher management positions.

Of course it is also true that, in any one country, it is the women with higher levels of schooling rather than those with lower schooling, who succeed in occupying decision-making positions. However, the evidence suggests that higher education relative to men does not improve women's occupation of these positions relative to men. All that can be said is that women's higher level of schooling improves their position relative to other women who have lower levels of schooling.

In short, the facts contradict the assumption that there is a correlation between level of schooling and women's empowerment.

This may be hard to grasp, since schools have educated us to believe that education is the means to advancement. We have been schooled to believe that men occupy decision-making positions because of their higher levels of schooling. The facts of the matter strongly suggest that men dominate decision-making positions because the patriarchal power structure puts them there and the patriarchal system discriminates against women who try to get into decision-making positions. Conventional schooling appears to be quite ineffective and irrelevant in changing this general pattern.

This has important implications for monitoring women's education. First, it means that our monitoring and evaluation should be directed at identifying the forms of education that lead to women's empowerment, rather than the forms of schooling that perpetuate subordination. For a start, it is important to distinguish skills training for self-advancement (within the patriarchal structure) from education for women's empowerment (for collective action to end discrimination and to close gender gaps).

Obviously it is not enough to monitor women's education by monitoring the output from all the courses and schools which choose to label themselves "women's education". Instead, there is a need to assess and monitor the quality of such provision, to assess whether it is concerned with schooling for subordination or education for empowerment. We need to formulate our own definition of women's education based on our own understanding of the sort of education that enables increased gender equality and women's empowerment.

Monitoring women's education must be equally about process and quality, as it is about outputs and quantity.

LIMITATIONS OF THE INPUT-OUTPUT MODEL OF EVALUATION

The considerations discussed above call into question whether an input-output model has much relevance for monitoring women's education. The value of quantitative monitoring of inputs and outputs is premised on the assumption that the process is appropriate. Once the process becomes the main focus of doubt and evaluation questions, then the model loses its usefulness. The original hope of a simple quantitative measure of progress falls away and is replaced by an interest in the quality of process.

The input-output model has no analytical power to monitor or evaluate the appropriateness and adequacy of the process. Instead, monitoring the quality of process requires very different concepts and methods, as have been introduced in this paper by means of the Women's Empowerment Framework. A process approach to monitoring and evaluating women's adult education programmes involves looking at whether the programme enables collective action for overcoming gender discrimination and women's occupation of decision-making positions.

From the empowerment perspective, it would be better to select, monitor, and evaluate those programmes with an empowerment element, to identify and develop those forms of education that can and do contribute to women's empowerment. From this point of view, process is more than a means to an end, because the empowerment is the essential part of the learning process and not merely an output of the process. Especially where lack of quality is currently the main problem, monitoring the quality of process becomes more important than monitoring the quantity of outputs.

CONCLUSION

No established method or "model" of monitoring and evaluation can be simply adopted in order to assess progress in women's adult education. Instead, existing models have to be adapted and new ones invented, if these are to fit our ideas of what women's education is and ought to be, what the purpose of women's education should be, and what constitutes progress.

If our monitoring is reduced to an interest in the technical and non-political details, without concern for the power dimensions, then how are we to monitor education as a means to women's empowerment? Rising enrolment figures may not show our increased education, but may instead be a sign of our increased accommodation and enslavement within the patriarchal system that discriminates against us. Such conventional programmes "educate" us to believe that the school has given us our chance, and subsequent failure is due to our own personal inadequacies.

However, the sisterhood needs to do more than take charge of the method and theory for monitoring and evaluating women's education. This must be part of the larger project of taking charge of women's education.

NOTES

1 These concepts and methods are taken from the materials developed by Longwe and Clarke for the evaluation of the gender orientation of development programmes, but they are here adapted for the special case of women's education programmes.

2 This framework was first published in Sara Longwe, 1991, "Gender Awareness: The Missing Element in a Development Project," in Candida March and Tina Wallace (Eds), *Changing Perceptions: New Writing on Gender and Development*, Oxfam.

3 Further a further discussion, see Sara Longwe, 1997, 'Education of Women's Empowerment or Schooling for Women's Subordination' in Carolyn Medel-Añonuevo (Ed), *Negotiating and Creating Spaces for Power*, UNESCO, Hamburg.

4 See Sara Longwe and Roy Clarke, 1999, *Towards Improved Leadership for Women's Empowerment in Africa*, African Leadership Forum (in press).

PART 1
Practices in Monitoring and Evaluating Literacy

WOMEN'S PARTICIPATION IN ADULT EDUCATION: THE IALS DATA[1]

Sofía Valdivielso Gómez

INTRODUCTION

Paolo Freire has said that "language and reality are dynamically interconnected. The comprehension achieved through critically reading a text implies perceiving the relationship between text and context." (Freire & Macedo, 1989). With this in mind, I am going to consider the importance of context in monitoring adult learning.

We are doubtless at a most historic moment in time, undergoing profound structural changes across the globe. The end of the century has been marked by deep fractures between tradition and modernity, North and South, and these affect each of the contexts in which we live. The development of new information technologies, rapid globalisation, the changing role of women, the "transformation of the intimacy" and of lifestyles, greater ecological consciousness, the close interdependence between the different social, political and economic spheres at the local, national, and international levels are but some of the significant changes we are experiencing today (Castells, 1994; Giddens, 1992).

In both the national and local contexts, universalization is causing, among other things, a segmentation of the labor market, which in turn is contributing to the process of social dualization whereby those excluded tend to be the educationally and culturally disadvantaged. At the same time, the transformation of the role of women has affected not only individuals but society as a whole. The number of women in the world who refuse to assume their traditional roles is increasing exponentially. The massive incorporation of women in the work force is restructuring the relationship between men and women. Nonetheless, there are still societies in which women continue to be considered less than nothing, which means we still have a long way to go.

Given this perspective, we may ask: Are we monitoring adult education in a way that measures participation? Are hegemonic forces shaping adult education? Which criteria should we apply in assessing adult learning? Are we considering extremely relevant variables such as unemployment, persecution, misogyny, paternalism, immigration, racism, and aging?

To answer some of these questions, I begin with the premise that all discourses are mediated by power relationships, making up a symbolic corpus that reaffirms and even legitimizes the separation between nations, social groups, gender, ethnic groups, workers and non workers, employed and unemployed, rich and poor, literate and illiterate. Rich nations extend their nets of cultural domination over poorer countries, perpetuating negative representations of the "the don't know". Thus, what is an unbearable inequality created by the differentiating dynamics of powerful nations and social classes has given way to a miserable dog-eat-dog society where everyone is responsible for his/her own individual destiny.

QUANTITATIVE OUTCOMES

I will now present some data from the International Adult Literacy Survey (IALS) conducted in two phases, the first in 1994 and the second in 1996. A total of twelve countries participated in the survey, namely, Australia, Belgium (Flanders), Canada, Ireland, the Netherlands, New Zealand, Poland, Sweden, Switzerland (both the German- and French- speaking communities), the United Kingdom, and the United States.

The goal of the survey was to obtain empirical data on participation and non-participation, reasons for participating or not participating, financing, provision, duration of the courses, places of learning, method of learning, etc. to gain a more in-depth knowledge of this field and to keep governments and international organizations informed on the decision-making process.

The same questionnaire was used in all the countries. The questionnaire was structured as a series of closed questions and answers. The analysis of responses reveals an initial picture of diversity and heterogeneity. In many western countries, participation in adult education and training is becoming the rule rather than the exception. The countries surveyed represent two extremes. The majority of the countries have a participation rate in education and training of around 40 percent for the twelve months preceding the survey. Belgium (Flanders) and Ireland make up a second group, with rates in the low 20s. (OECD & HRDC, 1997)

The adult education population is diverse, encompassing a wide range of ages, educational levels, income brackets, and social and cultural backgrounds. The patterns of participation reflect this diversity, which is present in each one of the countries taking part. However, within this diversity a homogeneous pattern develops. In all countries people with higher educational and income levels, who go to the cinema and theater more frequently, and who read more books, participated more than those who did not share these characteristics. Sweden is at the top, with a participation rate of 53 percent of the adult population. The lowest participation rate is in Poland, at 14 percent of the adult population.

A first general conclusion then would be that adult education in almost all the participating countries is acquired mostly by people of higher social status who are, in the first place, better educated. Thus, instead of reducing inequality, adult education seems to be compounding it.

Adults tend to register for a diverse range of educational programs. The quantitative data indicates that there is a tendency to choose courses related to work. In all the countries, except Sweden, men registered more than women for job-related courses, whereas more women than men signed up for courses related to their personal interests.

Another characteristic of adult education is the wide dispersion of the provision. In all the countries there is an enormous variety of providers. None of the countries had a provider which covered more than 30 percent of the national provision. In all the countries the primary providers are employers, while the public sector accounts for less than 10 percent of the general provision.

This suggests that because of scarce public supply, due in turn to structural adjustment policies, those who most need it find no route toward integration; instead they are excluded. The state has abandoned one of its basic functions: guaranteeing the right of all its citizens to learn. If this trend doesn't change, the 1997 Hamburg Conference declaration of principles concerning the right to learn will prove to be an empty promise for many social sectors.

As the private sector becomes the main provider, the concept of adult learning, which has been associated with social and individual transformation, will shift increasingly to training and the acquisition of skills.

The financial support that adults receive do vary. In Canada, the United States, the Netherlands, and Poland, the principal financial source mentioned by the participants is the employer. Everywhere, financial support from governmental and public sources is a distant third, after employers and self-support. In all the countries, except in Canada, no more than 14 percent of the learning projects are supported from public financial sources.

The patterns of financial support tend to differ between men and women. In all the countries, a greater proportion of courses or learning activities undertaken by women compared to men are financed by the participants themselves. Companies are not offering the same participation opportunities to women as to men. In Switzerland and in the Netherlands, men have 50 percent more chances than women to see their organized learning activities financed by their employer. We can conclude that the different participation patterns and rates are not due to the lack of motivation or interest of women, but to the scarce provision and the constraints to participation within the context of work.

The main provisions tend to be directed to men and include financial incentives, time sharing facilities, and motivational support. The majority of women, reflecting the gendered division of labor, tend to be employed in the secondary labor market where adult education programs may be more centered on employability than skill development. But at the same time, women tend to join programs on survival skills, on quality of life requirements, on empowerment, on communication skills, , often at their own expenses. More analyses are required to understand the difficulties encountered by women in their effort to adapt themselves to the changing requirements of labor markets and to use non-job-related training in their effort to integrate into the job market. Women, because they have less training opportunities, have fewer chances to find regular jobs. Because their job status is less secure, they have less chances to continue their education

Respondents who have not taken job-related courses were asked their reasons for not doing so. The first reason given both by men and women in all countries except in Poland is "lack of time", although this response must be interpreted carefully since it is well known that people tend to give "socially accepted" answers. The Polish women did not to participate primarily because it was "too expensive".

Gender differences are apparent in the second and third reasons given for not participating. "Too expensive" is the second reason generally expressed both by men and women, although the percentages vary considerably. For the Canadian, American and Polish respondents, the third reason for not participating is gave "family responsibilities" while for the Western European respondents this reason ranked sixth (Switzerland) and seventh (the Netherlands). However, in all of the countries "family responsibilities" are more important to females than to males. In the Netherlands, the fourth reason for women's non participation is "family responsibilities" while for men this ranked ninth; in the United States and Poland, it is third for women and seventh for men.

The differences in reasons "not to participate" given by men and women could be an indicator of a hidden discrimination. This discrimination is more subtle because it operates within the symbolic world of culture where the stereotype of the "good woman" and "family responsibilities" persist. The archetype of the traditional mother continues to condition the lives of many women, even those who enjoy economic independence. Economic independence for women does not necessarily equate with personal autonomy. Notions of democracy and symmetric relations within the family have not been adopted by every woman in Western countries. There is a growing number of women who develop new and more autonomous social relations, but there are still a great number of women who assume or tolerate traditional roles. For instance, many professional women think that the income they generate is less important than the one generated by their husband. Their relationship with men continues being defined by the traditional division of sexes. Even when the external conditions have changed, there remain many socio-cultural contexts in which women keep living in a traditional way. It is precisely in these traditional ways of living and thinking that many cultural barriers to participate can be found. Many women are struggling against these contradictions, and this may explain why they tend in all countries to look for courses that enhance their self-confidence and autonomy, and that teach different patterns of social participation and new ways of solving communication problems.

Qualitative Outcomes

The quantitative data from the IALS provide a static picture of social reality. In order to capture the inherent dynamism of social interaction—to identify subjects and actors, to explore notions of responsibility and freedom—we need to employ qualitative methodologies.

In the Canary Islands, we used the same questionnaire as the one used in the other participating countries, in two different situations: one in a survey of 2,000 people considered representative of the adult population over the age of 16, and another in discussion groups and in-depth interviews. In the questionnaire situation the person being surveyed chose one of the answers presented in the questionnaire whereas in the second situation only the questions were presented and the interviewee must formulate each answer.

Comparison of the results of the two test models proves very interesting. For example, when we presented the questionnaire in a discussion group to highly trained, well-educated professionals, they spontaneously provided answers which coincided with those published in the questionnaire. Some of the participants even expressed their answers using the very same terms as in the survey test. This was not the case when presenting the questionnaire to a group of less-educated people who were taking part in literacy and basic education courses. The answers provided by these people were more in keeping with other aspects not identified in the questionnaire.

The reasons given for taking part in the survey/discussions are dichotomized: professional or personal reasons. This classification is problematic because it forces the individual to choose between two options that are not mutually exclusive. This distinction between professional and personal reasons reflects a certain way of perceiving the world, which is not absolutely neutral, but rather indicates a clear class bias. For example, in a discussion group of middle-class professional participants in a foreign language course, the reasons for participating involved this distinction between the professional and personal aspects. So we received responses such as: "To obtain a specialization in some areas of my work, so I can do a better job..." "One of the courses was to get a promotion in my work and the other was for pleasure, as a hobby."

However, in a discussion group with persons of lower educational level, personal and professional reasons are mixed. The subjects do not feel divided between their professional and personal life because, among other things, many of the them are unemployed. For example, a 27-year-old male participant in a basic education course expressed the following:

> "My reasons involved seeing a 10-year-old child, ...with a pencil in his hand and he knew how to add things up correctly and then there's me with a job that I can do well and I don't know how to use a pencil. That was one of the things. ...Because of my work and my quality of life, really, to know that I can go anywhere and fill in any form or read a paper as well as anybody else..."

Or the response provided by a 51-year-old illiterate woman who is participating in a literacy program: "...I know... how wonderful it is to walk along the street and be able to read all the signs... and how sad it is when you have to say to someone: Excuse me, can you tell me how to get to a certain street and it turns out it's right there in front of you... but that's what happens when you do not know and you pass right by it..."

Quantitative data cannot tell us why things happen. Through discussion groups and in-depth interviews we can obtain more information. If we limit ourselves to strictly quantitative methods, then we miss the dynamics of interpersonal relationships. Combining qualitative and quantitative approaches may lead to a more comprehensive monitoring. An in-depth consideration of indicators is of little use if we are unable to understand what underpin social interaction.

The aim of any investigation is not simply to gain knowledge but also to provoke a range of analyses and discussions that help to generate responsive and transformative alternatives. In this sense, the role of the researcher in the process of monitoring in adult learning should not just involve managing a series of statistics, indicators or macrosurveys taken out of context. The central theme of the new research process should be to give all the actors a voice so that they consider themselves valued in each phase of the investigative process.

Some Conclusions

We have already seen how the current adult education picture is characterized by dispersed provision, diverse financial sources, and heterogeneity of participants. Given these, there is a need for information-gathering mechanisms in the field of adult learning. One such mechanism could be including some items on adult learning in the national census.

We also need good systems for monitoring the different courses being offered. In the formal system, the provision is always handed down by the ministries of education. They are responsible for ensuring everyone has the right to learn. In adult education, however, the ministry of education is not the only authority, nor is it the most important. Other ministries involved include health, social affairs, employment, etc. The state is also not the only provider. We find an enormous range of programs on offer organized by the private sector and by civil society groups.

The lack of coordination among different actors means that in a given territory we find different providers organizing the same courses for the same sector of the public.

This has led to a duplication of resources and expenses. This could be avoided by a better system of information and intercommunication among the sectors and actors so that what is offered is presented globally and not in bits and pieces.

On the other hand, the lack of information on the reality of adult learning causes public authorities to undervalue the work that is being done. We have seen how little money is invested by the state in these programs. This abdication by the state makes it difficult to guarantee education to broad social sectors, and fosters the imposition of market forces based on "user paying for culture". This in turn leads to the social exclusion of those who cannot pay. At this moment in our history, characterized by the dominance of neo-liberal policies, it is absolutely necessary to provide the fullest information possible in order to arrest this tendency and to obtain whatever resources are needed. We should develop systems of monitoring not merely of the necessities but also of the opportunities, not just of resources we need but also resources we already have; systems that are useful to the totality of society and not just to governments or employers. There are numerous resources that are wasted because they are not used, and they are not used because there is no information about their existence.

Similarly, it should provide information not only about participants, program availability and funding, but also about those who do not take part. Why are the people who most need the service the last to use it? What are the barriers to participation?

Finally, the universalistic tendencies and the processes of globalisation in which we are immersed require systems of information that encompass different nations and that facilitate dialogue and exchange of information between nations and peoples. The information generated by the monitoring of adult learning should provide answers, on a prioritized basis, about social inequalities, of which educational inequality is one of the indicators. It should also contribute to resolving some of the great problems of contemporary society, such as the struggle against racism, the promotion of human rights and fundamental freedoms, the recognition and strengthening of the equality between women and men, the maintenance and fostering of peace, and the preservation of our environment.

Adults interact in different social systems. Learning takes place in each of these systems. So it is necessary to provide systems of monitoring that are sufficiently flexible and open so as to be able to recognize these learning processes within an overall framework. A model of adult education capable of responding to the challenges that both people and societies currently face must bring together all the actors, facilitating synergy in the search for solutions.

We naturally ask ourselves, How can we do it? We believe it is possible to employ multiple perspectives in gathering information on what is happening locally and globally, on the micro as well as the macro situation, and on individual and social history.

The complex nature of reality pushes us forward and forces us to break away from the old positivist subject-object paradigm, which in most cases has led to the development of projects that proceed from the assumption that the project directors have a problem and we, the researchers and technicians, possess the solution. We must discard the ethnocentric attitude and think hermeneutically. In practice, this means realising that we all, men and women, have problems to solve and that collectively we can find solutions based on inter-subjective and inter-cultural dialogue.

In a society that is characterized by both greater segmentation and closer integration, the response to the situation of women must be local as well as universal, individual as well as generic. Our local ecosystem is intimately linked to the global ecosystem. Changes in one influence the other. This process requires an integral way of learning, a holistic conception of the being. Such an ecological vision is based on the notion of an interrelationship between the subject and her/his surroundings, both local and global. One is only able to discover the other, to see the differences and the similarities, if one is able to define herself or himself as an individual subject. The building of the self is a social process because one acquires significance only in relationship with other subjects. It is a process in which the boundaries between the workplace and the community are obscured.

I would like to end with a quote from Edgar Morin:

> "[I]t is not a matter of opposing the experience of living in favor of the theoretical abstraction, the social sciences over the exact sciences, philosophical reflection over scientific theory. It involves encouraging some people and others to get them to communicate... , multiplying interchanges and communications, so that all wandering off toward complexity comes together and thus, finally, we may conceive not only the complexity of every reality (physical, biological, human, sociological, political), but also the reality of complexity." (in Porlán, 1993: 54)

Works Cited

Castells, M. 1997. *La Era de la Informacion: Economia, Sociedad y Cultura*, Vol. 1 La Sociedad Red. Madrid: Alianza Editorial.

Freire, P. and Macedo, O. 1989. *Alfabetizacion: Lectura de la Palabra y Lectura de la Realidad*. Madrid: Paidos-MEC.

Giddens, A. 1992. *The Transformation of Intimacy: Sexuality, Love & Eroticism in Modern Societies*. Cambridge: Polity Press.

OECD & HRDC. 1997. *Literacy Skills for the Knowledge Society*. Paris and Ottawa: Organisation for Economic Co-operation and Development and Human Resources Development Canada.

Porlán, R. 1993. *Constructivismo y escuela. Hacia un modelo de enseñanza aprendizaje basado en la investigación*. Díada. Sevilla.

Notes

1 Most of the reflections presented in this paper were presented in CONFINTEA V jointly with Fernando López Palma.

MONITORING PARTICIPATION IN LITERACY AND CONTINUING EDUCATION: THE DHAKA AHSANIA MISSION EXPERIENCE

Ehsanur Rahman

THE ORGANISATION IN BRIEF

The Dhaka Ahsania Mission (DAM) is a non-government development organisation established in 1958 to serve the cause of humanity. Though it was established primarily as a philanthropic organisation, its agenda of activities has widened to cover diversified areas of socio-economic and cultural development with a view towards improving the life situation of disadvantaged groups. The package of development support services provided by DAM includes non-formal education for all age groups (children, adolescent and adults), continuing education at different levels including an equivalency programme, training, credit support for income generation, development of education and communication materials, environment conservation, support for human settlement, etc. In the formal education sector, DAM runs a training college for secondary school teachers, which offers a Bachelors Degree in Education, and a private university, the Ahsanullah University of Science and Technology. The target beneficiaries of DAM's development interventions are from the poorer sections in the community and, as a whole, women comprise more than 70 percent of the participants.

LITERACY AND CONTINUING EDUCATION PROGRAMMES

APPROACH AND COVERAGE

DAM considers education as the basic input in human resource development, and illiteracy as the root of poverty, underdevelopment and many of the social ills. Thus, DAM's development programme begins with education, follows with skill training, flourishes with income generation and continuing education, and ultimately results in environmentally sustainable programmes, absorbing disadvantaged children and others in the process.

The basic and continuing education programmes are implemented in a non-formal education setting. These programmes cover all age groups and have five components:

1) pre-primary education;

2) basic education for children;

3) literacy for adolescents;

4) adult literacy; and

5) continuing education.

Each of the programmes has been carefully designed to serve the needs of the relevant groups. Continuous review is undertaken to improve the programmes.

The objective of the adolescents' education programme is to provide illiterate boys and girls ages 11 to 14 with the necessary education, skill training, and awareness of various socio-economic fields in order to prepare them for their life ahead. The programme lasts for nine months and has a curriculum frame of three levels. Books for three grades and easy-to-read materials are provided as follow-up materials. Newsletters and wall magazines on local topics of interest to the neo-literate such as family life, social and legal issues, income generation activities, etc. are also supplied on a regular basis.

The literacy programme for adults consists of a series of activities leading to tangible economic gains. The nine-month programme is divided into two packages: six months cover the basic level, mid-level and self-learning level of literacy skills while the remaining three months are spent consolidating the literacy skills acquired. The functional aspects incorporated in the reading materials of the programme cover family life, income generation, organisation building, and civic consciousness. Simultaneous to learning basic literacy skills, graded easy-to-read materials that contain topics that interest the learners in their day-to-day life are supplied.

The continuing education programme is implemented for both neo-literate adults and adolescents through a system of community libraries, known as Ganokendra. These are really the village community centres with a library and facilities for games and other socio-cultural activities. The neo-literate participates in regular discussions on issues of local interest. Ganokendra are located in locally built houses to which the learners and the local people have easy access. Follow-up and easy-to-read materials containing topics that interest the learners, wall magazines, literacy follow-up books, and daily newspapers are supplied to these Ganokendra.

As of February 1999, 122,875 learners in 4,274 centres have participated in the DAM Literacy Programme. There are 873 continuing education centres to reinforce the literacy and functional skills of the neo-literate.

Programme Management and Supervision

There is a field set-up linked with the programme desk at the central office of the organisation. At the bottom of the field set-up is the facilitator. Facilitators remain in constant touch with the learners. Above them are field organizers or supervisors. They are responsible for organizing and supervising the learning centres. One supervisor usually oversees 15 learning centres. Supervisors and facilitators are responsible for involving the community in conducting baseline surveys, identifying beneficiaries, organising learning centres, and mobilising resources. The supervisors visit centres once a week, during which they look into the teaching/learning process, attendance, dropout rate, community participation, use of materials, and learners' achievement level.

Above the supervisors are the area coordinators or assistant area coordinators. One (assistant) area coordinator supervises the work of five supervisors. Area coordinators or assistant area coordinators are responsible for field level implementation of the programmes. They report directly to the programme officer. Programme officers, the team leaders for programme implementation, get back-up support from the programme coordinator and the director.

The programme management line-up is shown in the following organogram.

Head Office level	Director (Programmes)
	Programme Coordinator
	Programme Officer
	↑↓
Field Level	Area Coordinator/ Assistant Area Coordinator
	Supervisor
	Facilitator ←→ Centre Management Committee

All officers/personnel have defined responsibilities in monitoring project implementation. Upon enrolment every learner is given an identification number. With this, any learner not attending sessions or lagging behind can easily be identified, and corrective measures taken. The facilitators and the supervisors liase closely with each learner's household to improve attendance and reduce dropouts.

The core learning materials used in the centres were designed and developed by the Materials Development Division of DAM. One of the most important features of these primers is a built-in learner assessment device which allows for the assessment of the learner's progress at any time during the course. Monthly assessments of the learners are conducted by teachers, supervisors and area coordinators, and a terminal test for each level/grade of each programme component is given.

Monitoring of Literacy and Continuing Education in DAM

Monitoring System

DAM has a built-in monitoring system for programmes under implementation. Monitoring indicators are set in line with the programme objectives. In monitoring literacy and continuing education programmes, the central office is linked to the lowest implementation units and the grassroots level. The facilitators, supervisors, area coordinators, and programme officers all have their defined roles in collecting information and giving feedback at regular intervals. Three types of monitoring tools are used: reporting forms, field visit reports, and record books. Findings are collected through field visits, focused group discussions, learner assessment, and reports from centre committee leaders, facilitators, supervisors, coordinators, and monitoring personnel

DAM's monitoring system takes into account the following needs:
- to get information about delivery of input
- to examine the process of implementation
- to assess the participation of learners and the community
- to initiate corrective measures in and prompt response to problem situations
- to assess output
- to facilitate effective planning and informed decision-making

The general objectives of monitoring are
a. to collect quantitative and qualitative information from the field;
b. to check the activities of the programmes as per objectives; and
c. to provide feedback for management decision-making.

Broad areas of monitoring include basic information, attendance, progress, teaching-learning method, supply and use of materials, supervision, personnel, and financial management. Routine output tables provide a number of basic progress data about coverage, attendance, learning achievement, supervision and dropout. Basic information reports include class information summaries, teacher information summaries, supervisor information summaries, and learner information summaries. Attendance reports include the average attendance of learners per class and the attendance record of facilitators. Learning progress reports explain grades achieved by learners, skills achieved by learners, gap between teaching and learning, and progress of learners as per target. Reports on supervision include number and frequency of visit, issues supervised, and findings from visits. Dropout reports summarize the rates of and the reasons for dropout.

> **Examples of Monitoring Areas (extracted from some MIS reports)**
>
> *Continuing Education Centre* (MIS Report 70, November 1998)
> - total number of members and ratio of active members (defined in terms of attendance)
> - percentage of members who borrow books (as per sample check)
> - whether wall magazine is produced by the centre
> - participation in management committee meetings and decision-making
> - local collection of resource materials (books, game materials, information materials)
> - types of socio-cultural programmes organised, classified under the following headings:
>   - open discussions
>   - recreational events
>   - sports
>   - resolving any social crisis
>   - religious functions
>   - observation of important days
>   - health services
> - percentage of neo-literates who have access to credit support
> - members in gender development training
> - members in environment training
>
> *Group Management* (MIS Report 67, November 1998)
> - organisation of issue-based meetings at group level
> - types of decisions made and followed up
> - awareness level of group management committee members about their role
> - initiatives by the group to make the group self-reliant

A cross analysis of the output generated in monitoring reveals a correlation between the different factors identified, e.g., learners' attendance, supervision, teachers' qualification, parental education age. All basic information about learners, facilitators, and programme personnel are disaggregated according to gender. Analysis of monitoring data relating to participation and progress is made from a gender perspective. Here are a few examples of gender-focused analysis tables.

- Analysis of learners' progress by gender
- Analysis of learners' attendance by gender
- Analysis of learners' attendance by teachers' gender
- Analysis of parents' participation in meeting by gender
- Analysis of reason for dropout by gender
- Analysis of learners' drop out by teachers' gender

Feedback on the monitoring findings is given regularly through written communication and discussion meetings. The monitoring personnel, on the basis of their field visit findings, send feedback to the field offices and central programme personnel in writing. Data generated from routine reports are analysed by both monitoring personnel and programme personnel, according to their own needs. Feedback is given on the progress, level of participation, quality of information (consistency, reliability, timeliness, etc.), as well as possible actions to be taken to address the limitations of the programme.

Monitoring Indicators

Monitoring indicators, both micro and macro, are identified during project planning. These are developed consistently with the project objectives, taking into account the issues to be monitored at both macro and micro levels. At the macro level, planning and management aspects are covered. However, learners' progress and participation are given equal emphasis. At the learning centre level, indicators are set to monitor classroom environment, learning process, achievement, community participation, availability of learning materials, etc. Though there are common sets of indicators, project-specific indicators are identified to monitor specific interventions planned through a project. Examples of macro and micro indicators are given below.

Micro Indicators (used mostly for field monitoring):

- Coverage of target learners with breakdown from socio-economic and gender background
- Average attendance by gender
- Learning process (To what extent participatory?)
- Access of learners to education materials and use of supplementary materials
- Achievement of learners in terms of literacy and functional skills
- Drop out rate with major reasons of dropout
- Input from community organisation (if any) to run the centre
- Visit of centre by local extension agency personnel
- Visit by centre management people or local leaders
- Practical use of literacy and functional skills and change observed in the family
- Teachers' initiative for community resource mobilisation
- Completion rate in basic literacy and linkage to continuing education
- Social/cultural events organised at learning centre level
- Types of locally procured information, education and communication materials

Macro Indicators (used mostly for macro management):

- Planned learners covered
- Completion rate and major reasons for drop out

Achievement level of learners in terms of national curriculum

Training contents and coverage for facilitators, supervisors and coordinators

Supervision frequency and issues

Participation of community organisation

Input for and by the community organisation in the programme

Improvement in organisational capacity of community organisations

Major problems in terms of participation of learners, particularly women/ working adolescents

Availability of funds and utilisation

Issues covered in continuing education

Rate of participation of neo-literate in continuing education

Extent of community contribution in making continuing education sustainable

---

Examples of Project-based Indicators

Project 1: Education and Financial Services for Neo-literate Women

Post-literacy
- provision for literacy practice of adults, adolescents and children through establishment of Ganokendra (People's Centre) and enrolment for further education
- supply of information, education and communication (IEC) materials to the Ganokendra on a regular basis
- participation of neo-literate adults, adolescents and children in Ganokendra activities/continuation of education of graduates of literacy centres
- undertaking of different community activities by the Ganokendra
- community management of the Ganokendra
- change in attitude of the beneficiaries
- impact of the programme on the community

Socio-cultural development
- training provided on gender development
- training provided on leadership
- women's participation in decision-making
- cultural programme organised by the Ganokendra

Environment preservation
- organisation of environment volunteer groups
- activities of the group on environment awareness
- plants supplied, planted and surviving
- ovens made and their usage

Participation of Stakeholders and Its Monitoring

Monitoring access of downtrodden, hard to reach women, their retention and participation in the dialogue at learning centre level and at the social level are considered key areas of participation under DAM's existing literacy and continuing education programmes.

Participation is seen as a three-step process—motivation, mobilisation and action. It is important that all stakeholders in literacy and continuing education—learners, facilitators, supervisors, community organisations, government, and other development agencies—are motivated towards the cause of literacy/continuing education. But motivation alone is not enough. All have to be ready to help implement the program, including mobilising available resources. Finally, stakeholders must physically participate in programme activities to ensure the success of the programme. The monitoring system of DAM has been designed to determine the level of participation of relevant persons or organisations in the planning, delivery and management of programmes.

Project 2: Improvement of Water and Sanitation Conditions in Rural Areas

Macro-indicators
- whether the community has become aware of the need for and benefits of safe water and good sanitation, improved knowledge of health and hygiene, and a cleaner environment
- whether the community's attitude towards using sanitary latrines (as opposed to defecating out in the open) and safe water has changed
- whether the demand for safe water and sanitary latrines has increased and the people try to meet this demand using their own resources

Some micro-indicators
- community owns the tubewell with safe water
- women caretakers maintain the tubewell
- family members share water collection from the tubewell
- reduction in water- and sanitation-related diseases
- other water sources like ponds are protected from pollution
- all family members use sanitary latrine
- all latrines are fenced
- latrine pans are clean
- cleaning of latrine pans are done by all adult members in the family
- latrine production centres are within easy reach of available transport
- women are managing the latrine production centres
- women are playing an active role in decision-making regarding health and sanitation practices in the family

LEARNERS' PARTICIPATION

Learners' participation in planning involves identifying issues for learning, locating centre houses, setting times for classes, and planning follow-up programmes. Though the basic literacy primers are pre-set, there is provision for supply of supplementary learning materials that suit the needs of the learners. These are either DAM-supplied or collected locally. The learners choose the types of materials they need and contribute in developing materials for local use. The learners also play a key role in increasing participation of fellow learners. Since in class they work in small groups, a sort of group cohesion is developed and the group members try to ensure the attendance of other members.

Learners are represented in the centre management committee. The committee looks after local management aspects of the centre and meets on a monthly basis to review programme activities. Participation of learners in class and management committee meetings are monitored through routine reports, while their participation in planning centres and the selection of learning materials are done through discussion with them during field visits by monitoring personnel.

> **Extract from the 1998-1999 Annual Report of the project, "Education and Financial Services for Neo-literate women"**
>
> The books and booklets, posters and stickers used in the Ganokendra are collected from internal and external sources. Books and IEC materials on diversified fields are made available to these centres. Books and materials supplied contain many information for agriculture, poultry farming, livestock raising, kitchen gardening, small business management, running of co-operatives, environment and sanitation, health and hygiene, food and nutrition, dangers of drug addiction and a variety of other fields of interest to the readers including comics and stories. Ganokendra are organised and managed by the neo-literate groups in collaboration with the local community through a committee formed with five to seven members. There is contribution from the members for construction of the house, procurement of materials and socio-cultural activities.

The types of materials selected for continuing education by the neo-literates are summarised in a recent evaluation report: "Graduates made requests that more materials be supplied from time to time. They mentioned that reading materials particularly relating to the holy Quoran, sayings of the prophets, prayer practices, life sketches of nobles, health and child care are needed in the centre as post-literacy materials." Materials supplied to the centres are monitored on a monthly basis.

PARTICIPATION OF FACILITATORS

The facilitators, most of whom are women, actively participate in the selection of houses and setting times for classes. They also collect and supply supplementary learning materials. The facilitators also help develop learner-generated materials for use in the centres. Besides conducting classes, they pay home visits as part of rapport-building with the irregular learners and to increase the rate of participation and prevent dropout. The centre teacher works as the member secretary in the centre management committee and coordinates local management aspects of the centre. Regular participation of the facilitators in class and participation of management committee members in centre management are monitored through routine reports. Information is collected on regularity of meetings, participation rate, issues discussed, the role of the committee in resource mobilisation, and problem resolution. Participation of teachers in planning centres and selection of learning materials are monitored through discussion with them during field visits by monitoring personnel.

A major source of data on the effectiveness of adult education programmes are focused group discussions. Discussion sessions are held separately with graduates, family heads, officials, and local leaders in different programme sites. A recent programme evaluation report, for example, says, "... meetings with graduates of all three academic sessions were held at all locations—Satkhira, Debhata and Kaliganj. All the groups were composed of 15 graduates, five from each year. All the groups except one were composed of female groups. There was one mixed group at Kaliganj. The discussions that ensued were free and lively."

COMMUNITY PARTICIPATION

Community members help the facilitators and other field officials in identifying illiterates in the programme area, establishing centre houses, and forming centre management committees. They also help mobilise local resources, particularly for establishing centre houses. It should be noted that the learning centres are organised in community-contributed houses. The committee members from the community also help motivate irregular learners to attend classes. Some members visit the centres and provide instant support. Participation of the community is monitored through routine reports, reviews, and field visits. Information is collected on regularity of meetings, participation rates, issues discussed, the role of the committee in resource mobilisation, and problem resolution.

PARTICIPATION OF SUPERVISORS.

The role of supervisors is to provide back-up support in planning and running literacy and continuing centres. They work hand-in-hand with the facilitators and other grassroots level actors in identifying learning needs, available resources, and potential facilitators. They maintain close ties with the centre management committee and with local leaders. They organise training courses for facilitators and centre committee leaders. The supervisors visit the learning centres on a weekly basis and provide instant support to the facilitators. Central level personnel monitor participation of the supervisors through reports of activities and field visits. Issues covered in monitoring are frequency of visits to centres, issues visited and feedback given, local resource mobilisation, regularity of local coordination meetings, issues discussed, and problems addressed.

ROLE OF COMMUNITY ORGANISATIONS

Community organisations play a very important role in implementing literacy programmes in certain districts of DAM's programme areas. In these districts DAM implements programmes through community-based local organisations. DAM provides technical and materials support while the local organisation implements the programmes. The objective of this strategy is to develop the capacity of local organisations to implement literacy and continuing education programmes, so that in the future these organisations would be able to join national literacy programmes. Aside from the micro-areas of monitoring mentioned above, initiatives of local organisations in community mobilisation, resource mobilisation, linking of learners with current programmes of the organisation, and the role of local orgranisations in coordination meetings are also monitored. Monitoring of these aspects are done interactively in the monthly coordination meetings. In addition, the monitoring personnel give feedback on the basis of their findings on organisational management issues.

Responsibility of local NGOs in implementing literacy projects
(Extract from the DAM-LNGO partnership agreement for the project, "Capacity-Building for Basic and Continuing Education")

- making the project implementation plan
- conducting a baseline survey and identifying illiterate learners
- selecting facilitators and organising their training in collaboration with DAM
- procuring materials from DAM and supplying the centres
- mobilising the local community, parents and learners to join hands with the programme
- supervising learning centres
- organising continuing education centres and linking up the learners to ensure literacy practice

---

Role of Other Agencies

Development agencies and government extension departments play a very crucial role in the improvement of the quality of life of the learners. DAM wants to develop the link between field level personnel from these organisations and the learning centres. This is accomplished by organising visits of extension personnel to the centres and arranging supply of IEC materials from these departments/organisations to the centres. DAM field officials and facilitators organise issue-based discussions in the learning centres and invite these extension personnel to guide the discussion. Moreoever, information materials are collected, at the initiative of individual personnel, and are used in the centres. Frequency of visits, issues discussed, and number and types of materials supplied to the centres are monitored on a monthly basis.

HOW PARTICIPATION CONTRIBUTES TO WOMEN EMPOWERMENT

Empowerment is seen as a process that enables the participants to make decisions relating to various aspects of their lives. In other words, an empowered person can take full control of his/her life and make informed decisions. Empowerment of women involves developing their skills and attitudes to enable them to overcome poverty, improve their quality of life, and attain full development. It equips them to understand their situation by developing their critical thinking.

Active participation in DAM learning centres have brought about remarkable changes in the lives of the women learners. They have developed self-respect and confidence. They have become income earners and have started to adopt new and improved farm practices. They have become conscious of issues such as health, environment and sanitation, and have started to organise programmes on their own. The marriage of young girls has been delayed in most cases. Those with children have started to send their children to school. These women are increasingly assuming decision-making roles in the family as well as in society. Moreover, mutual respect, understanding and cooperation between the male and female members of the family have noticeably deepened. All these developements have given the women hope for a better life. (DAM Annual Report, 1994)

In order to evaluate the overall impact of the programme on the lives of the women, their psychological well-being is assessed at the end of the project. One such evaluation uses a five-point Likert scale measuring four dimensions, i.e., self-confidence, self-esteem, conscious thinking, and life satisfaction, in a total of 12 items. The highest possible score is 60 and the lowest, 12. High scores are indicative of a positive psychological state. The average well-being score of graduates of the 12-month adult literacy programme from different areas ranges from 44.46 to 46.64.

> **Extract from the December 1998 Progress Report of the project, "Functional Education through Local Initiatives (Phase II)"**
>
> In the centres, the learners formed issue-based study groups to read and discuss the text. These issues were also carried over for discussion in the group level meetings for undertaking actions towards socio-economic development. The teachers and supervisors have assessed learners' progress on a regular basis.
>
> In addition to literacy learning, the learners organised socio-cultural activities on different occasions. For example, on national immunisation day and on the days of distribution of vitamin A capsules by the local health departments, learners from adult centres took initiatives to ensure participation of peoples. An anti-drug campaign was also organised in some villages; various health-related issues have been taken up for discussion in the classes, in parents meetings, and in the meetings of the centre management committee.

LESSONS LEARNED

A full review of existing adult literacy programmes of development agencies must be undertaken in order to determine whether current packages contribute to women empowerment, whether the programme is accessible to the poor population, and whether women's participation is ensured. More important is the relevance of the content of the learning materials. Materials must address the immediate learning needs of the people, particularly in relation to women empowerment.

The needs of the unreached population are such that they can be effectively addressed only when the learners are made to "own" the programmes and actively participate in their own learning. This means that participation cannot be ensured unless the learning and living needs of the target beneficiaries are integrated both in the materials and in the actual conduct of the programme. The challenge in organising learning sequences around actual life concerns of the learners can only be met when there is a shared perception among the learners, the facilitators, and the community of the core purposes of the programme and the learning materials.

Learning sequences built around the basic needs of the poor are best formulated by organising learning around the learners' own activities, contextualising learning by drawing from learners' experience, and involving learners in decision-making about their learning and other affairs. Treating the learners as passive receptacles of information from the teacher or the textbook will not fullfill the critical learning needs of learners, who for many reasons have had no prior education. What is required is a teaching-learning strategy that puts the learners at the centre of an interactive process. Appropriately developed learning materials can be effective tools to facilitate these sorts of learning. The demand for "appropriateness" should lead programme managers and materials developers to look for innovative materials. Innovation should be in terms of both content and method of learning, the latter being largely influenced by the format of the materials.

Once a participatory programme package is designed, the next important task is to revisit the monitoring indicators to check whether they address adequately the concerns of gender development: whether the programme equips women to live on equal footing with men and to participate actively in community activities; whether it promotes self-reliance among the women in all aspects of their life—social, political, economic, cultural; whether it enables the women to make their own choices; and whether it develops in the women the ability to cope with changes in their context, thus to continuously improve their quality of life.

THE RENÉ MOAWAD FOUNDATION EXPERIENCE IN LEBANON

Fady Yarak

INTRODUCTION

Before its 16-year civil war, Lebanon was considered a model of access to education and gender equity in education in the Middle East. But this small country of 10,452 sq. km overlooking the Mediterranean and a population of around three and half million is now emerging from a war that has destroyed its economy and infrastructure.

Some 450,000 of the population are displaced and living under difficult conditions, deprived of their basic needs. In addition, Israeli military actions in the South and West Bekaa continue to displace families from their homes and communities. The situation is further complicated by rural-to-urban migration which disrupts the economy, disintegrates the social and family network, and leads to the growth of poverty belts in the cities, accompanied by high unemployment rates and in some cases by the rise of drug abuse. These communities are a fertile soil for radical ideologies, delinquency, and prostitution.

In 1993, the government announced a US$13 billion reconstruction plan aimed at rehabilitating Lebanon's physical infrastructure and stimulating economic development. However, the plan had no clear strategy or comprehensive view of social development. Indeed, rapid post-war development has resulted in an unequal distribution of wealth. Estimates indicate that over 35 percent of Lebanese families live below the poverty line, with three-quarters of them residing in remote rural and peri-urban areas. Indicators seem to point to increasing disparities between social groups and geographical regions, which in turn increases the vulnerability of households and forces more children into difficult situations, such as child labor, school dropout, etc.

The fighting has also taken its toll on mental and social welfare in the country, including the educational system. The damage done to the educational system is difficult to gauge, as accurate current data are scarce and often contradictory. UNICEF reports that enrolment has decreased since the outbreak of the war, with about 30 percent of Lebanese children not attending primary school. Studies also show alarming dropout rates.

Illiterates make up 11.1 percent of the whole population and 19 percent of the adult population. It is worth noting, however, that illiteracy is concentrated in the older age groups, particularly among women above 40 years of age at 46 percent compared to 22.1 percent for men. Moreover, 67.3 percent of illiterates are rural poor. Illiteracy rates are the highest and educational deprivation is greatest in North Lebanon.

Education in Lebanon has the following features:

1. shifted national priorities resulting in limited focus of financial or personal resources on the educational sector;
2. weakened national and educational infrastructure;
3. declining girls' enrollment at the primary level;
4. low enrollment for boys and girls at the secondary level; and
5. illiteracy among women, particularly in rural areas.

CURRENT EFFORTS IN EDUCATION

Lebanon has embarked on a process of healing and reconstruction in which the government, the private sector, non-governmental organizations (NGOs), international agencies, and individuals are all playing a significant part. As part of this process, there have been concerted efforts to address the issue of education. Some initiatives were more successful than others.

The International Convention on the Rights of the Child has been certified and a number of institutional mechanisms, mainly a parliamentary commission for child rights, have been put in place at both the governmental and non-governmental levels. A law was adopted in 1996 raising the minimum age for work from eight to 14 years. It is expected that a national strategy for fighting child labor will be completed in 1999 by the Ministry of Labor in collaboration with other ministries and NGOs. Another law rendering basic education until the age of 12 years free and compulsory was enacted in March 1998.

In January 1998, the Ministry of Labor issued recommendations concerning underaged children in the labor force, including a permanent media campaign to spread awareness, an increase in the penalties for employers who hire underaged children, compulsory education, vocational training programmes and workshops, the development of rural industries to create employment opportunities, the ratification of international conventions, and most importantly the implementation of the conventions ratified by the Lebanese government.

The Ministry of Education has also initiated reform of the educational curricula and improvement of monitoring systems at school level to reduce dropouts. School counselors have been trained to diagnose children with problems at school. Nevertheless, the system is in need of further fine-tuning if dropout rates are to be effectively reduced. Accelerated vocational training and education has been initiated by the government to empower working children, 95 percent of whom aged ten to 13 years are illiterate.[1]

At the end of 1995, the Lebanese government formed the National Literacy Committee under the supervision of the Ministry of Social Affairs, and consisting of representatives from various ministries and NGOs. Unfortunately, three years after its formation the Committee has only been able to present a five-year plan of action, the implementation of which is still pending.

There have been notable efforts by civil society, particularly by NGOs representing a variety of perspectives on women and education. Although the impact of these NGOs cannot be denied, problems remain in their approach to gender issues. Moreover, there is a lack of coordination among these different groups.

SOME CONSTRAINTS IN GIRLS' EDUCATION

The data for some basic indicators related to women education and participation in development are not disaggregated by gender. However, some of the statistics show that girls constitute a disproportionate share of the unreached population. Available data suggest that the girls most in need are those in the rural, poor or most culturally restricted areas.[2]

There are a number of educational, economic, cultural, and political constraints to girls obtaining an education.

EDUCATIONAL CONSTRAINTS

The main constraint in education for girls is lack of access. The shortage of schools, teachers, books, materials, and equipment contribute to lowering girls' enrolment. In rural areas, where girls are more likely to miss class due to agricultural or households chores, girls may drop out to avoid repeating or catching up. The absence of female teachers is also a major constraint, particularly at the secondary level.

Economic constraints

Girls are also likely to be out of school for economic reasons. Lack of money for fees is usually listed as the primary reason for dropping out. Scholarships, uniforms, books, and reduced fees are also listed as the most important incentives for school persistence. For many families, the direct cost of school supplies, materials, and transportation far outweigh the benefits of having girls educated. In lower income and agricultural families, the loss of girls' labor in the home and the field is an opportunity cost that families cannot afford. And where the demand for domestic help is greater than for skilled or educated workers, education is considered unimportant and useless.

Cultural constraints

Cultural factors play a highly significant role in girls' participation. In addition to financial constraints, parental reluctance is an important deterrent to girls' persistence. Many communities, especially rural ones, do not value education for girls for its own sake. In addition, when daughters reach puberty, many parents find mixed-sex classrooms and male teachers undesirable. Age at marriage is also a factor in rural areas. Marriage at an early age takes priority over keeping girls in school. Another cultural constraint is the overall low status of women. Male decision-makers may not value female participation at the learning or decision-making levels. All of these factors contribute to an intergenerational cycle of female illiteracy that is hard to break.

Political constraints

The political situation in Lebanon has a significant impact on education in general, and girls' education in particular. Civil war, political violence, armed conflict, and political instability have serious consequences for female education, specifically in terms of continuity of schooling.

The René Moawad Foundation Adult Literacy Programme

After several years working in North Lebanon, it became clear to the Rene Moawad Foundation or RMF that illiteracy was an obstacle to the advancement and empowerment of women. Field staff estimate that over 40 percent of the mothers of children benefiting from RMF mobile clinics are illiterate. Furthermore, a younger generation of girls who leave school as early as the age of thirteen was growing.

In response to this, the RMF adopted a literacy programme initiated by the local community. The goals of this literacy programme are:

1) overcome gender, rural/urban disparities in literacy and education;

2) offer women better opportunities and life chances;

3) empower women through knowledge and encourage them to be active members of the community;

4) reach the whole family, which is the basic unit in our social structure, by educating the mother;

5) allow women to express their interests, needs and concerns;

6) enable women to play an active role in family decision-making;

7) enable women to participate in the process of sustainable development; and

8) provide a free space for women to interact and discuss common interests and concerns, such as gender violence.

The programme was designed to cover nine months and the curricula divided into three levels: for beginners to learn basic reading and grammar; for intermediate learners to be able to keep accounts and to continue improving their reading skills; and for advanced learners to be able to read newspapers and help their children with their homework.

The literacy manual, "Taalam, Taharar (Learn, Get Free)," developed in 1994 by the Save the Children Foundation (SCF), Terre des Hommes, and the Ecumenical Popular Educational Programme using the Freirean approach, was used in these classes. However, there were problems with the manual as it was not gender sensitive and was not appropriate to the local cultural context. Another weakness was its reliance on the literacy facilitator in the absence of supplementary activities. By 1996 another manual had been developed by UNICEF in collaboration with the Ministry of Social Affairs. However, it only covers basic literacy and is not very innovative in introducing basic concepts related to life skills, health or women's roles. Moreover, the cost of the manual—US$7—is prohibitive.

The first class that was formed by the RMF in 1993 included 12 women, mostly mothers of children in the village public school. The session was led by a female teaching in the public school but who was not from the village. This proved to be an advantage as instruction from her was more readily accepted by the women than if she were a local.

In 1994, the RMF began another literacy programme in collaboration with SCF-US. Ten classes were opened in Akkar, North Lebanon, a region with the highest illiteracy rate in the country. Around 150 participants between the ages of 15 and 45 attended these classes twice a week, two hours per session. This Level I literacy course lasted nine months, at the end of which participants were able to read and write basic Arabic.

From 1995 to 1996, three literacy training workshops were conducted to enhance and upgrade the skills of literacy facilitators. The first workshop aimed at acquainting the literacy facilitators with the literacy manual. The second workshop introduced teachers to different teaching techniques, e.g., developing a lesson plan and supplementary activities, creating a participatory atmosphere in the classroom. The third literacy workshop dealt with the question of the formation of a literacy class and its relation to dropouts. The workshop speaker stressed the importance of the human relationship between the facilitator and the learner. Dialogue and discussion were also presented as the key to the success of a literacy class. The need for follow-up on the skills learned in Level I as well as the development of functional literacy, i.e., Level II literacy, was addressed briefly. The larger role of the facilitator in Level II and the need for facilitators to continue their own education, mainly through reading, were also discussed.

From 1996 to 1997, the RMF conducted 14 Level I classes, reaching approximately 200 women. These were funded by the RMF and the Canadian Bureau of International Education. In acknowledgment of its continuing efforts in the field of literacy, the RMF was made a member of the National Literacy Committee. The RMF defined its literacy strategy, thus

In terms of advocacy:

1. actively participate in the National Literacy Committee
2. play an effective role in the Children's Right Committee to insure compulsory primary education and activate laws regulating child labor.

In terms of capacity-building:

1. train and supervise educational staff
2. train facilitators on adult education

In terms of service delivery:

1. expand the scope of activities in order to reach more of the population

In terms of empowerment:

1. provide women, especially heads of households, with basic life skills in order to promote their role in development.

All the facilitators are women who share similar backgrounds (social, economic, environmental, etc.) with the beneficiaries. This creates a strong bond based on the sharing and exchange of experiences between teacher and student.

From 1997 to 1998, the RMF worked closely with OXFAM GB to mainstream gender into its literacy programme and to integrate it into other activities. The educational staff and the facilitators attended a workshop on gender and tried to apply their new knowledge directly in the field in four pilot classes. OXFAM GB and the RMF also developed some indicators to assess the impact of the classes and training on the beneficiaries.

Input Indicators

- ability to find funding for gender mainstreaming in literacy
- government perception of gender mainstreaming in literacy

Process Indicators

- beneficiaries' views of new approaches to literacy
- enrolment rates in classes
- dropout rates
- active participation of both facilitators and beneficiaries
- field implementation of gender and literacy classes

Output Indicators

- knowledge of the importance of gender relations by both participants and facilitators
- improved gender content of literacy curriculum
- integration of the gender perspective into other literacy curricula
- improved status of women beneficiaries and facilitators
- creation of social support networks among women

Moreover, the RMF collaborated with the World Health Organization National AIDS Programme to incorporate health messages in the literacy or vocational training sessions, especially on sexually transmitted diseases and AIDS. The facilitators, after attending a training workshop on these issues, produced a manual for literacy facilitators of NGOs working in adult education.

The activities planned by the RMF for 1998 to 1999 respond to the needs identified in field studies as well as to those that emerged as the organization's work evolved. These activities will address all three fields of women work—productive, reproductive, and community.

Mainstreaming gender into literacy and vocational training

Literacy and vocational training sessions will be adapted so as to address gender issues, such as gender-biased distribution of resources, institutionalized gender discrimination, etc. These activities will address the productive as well as the community aspect of women's work. Reading and writing will allow the women to participate more actively and efficiently in various community events, e.g., elections, committees, fora, etc. Vocational training will improve the skills that women already have and teach them new income-generating skills.

Integrating reproductive health into the different programmes

This will address the third field of women work—reproductive duties. The health awareness programme informs women on vital health issues, such as reproductive health, hygiene (personal and environmental), sexually transmitted diseases, AIDS, etc. These issues are directly related to the health and survival of the women's families.

Discussing issues related to the economy of the rural families.

The knowlwedge gained from these discussions will enable women to obtain micro-credits, run small enterprises, and keep accounts.

Constraints

Despite improvements over the years, the literacy programme still needs more direction and clarification. Education staff should be trained to train other facilitators all over the country and to monitor and evaluate the programme in-depth. Another constraint is the lack of Level II materials. Other areas for improvement are:

- Giving further training to education staff and community facilitators.

- Developing functional literacy by integrating with other programmes like credit and early childhood messages.

- Developing supplementary materials and activities which teach skills that the participants can apply in their daily lives, e.g., filling up application forms, reading manuals, running a business, etc.

- Developing participatory women-focused materials for Level II literacy classes (The education department is in the process of developing some materials of this nature.).

- Securing funding, since until now the RMF operates on a yearly basis without continuity or security for the future.

The RMF Vision for Literacy

In the years since the literacy programme began, the RMF has come to realize the need to direct its efforts towards maintaining the skills acquired by the neo-literate women. This requires the incorporation of follow-up programmes, including the development of post-literacy materials and the integration of more participants into other activities such as joining women's groups, vocational training, access to credit programmes. By doing so, the RMF hopes to reduce the loss of skill and increase retention rates.

The RMF is now seeking to share this experience with other NGOs working in similar impoverished and marginal settings so as to promote literacy as a vehicle for addressing gender inequality.

Works Cited

1 UNICEF and Ministry of Social Affairs. 1997. "Child Labor in Lebanon."

2 UNICEF, Basic Services Project.

THE WOMEN IN ENTERPRISE DEVELOPMENT (WED) PROJECT:
MONITORING AND EVALUATION PRACTICES

Myrna Lim

INTRODUCTION

Today's world is a world of changes. And these are interesting times for those of us in development work and the educational sector. In countries all over the world, education at all levels is now under review. This is true in developed countries but more so in a developing country like the Philippines. More than ever before, the critical importance of education in developing the full potential of people, is being recognized. Today, the call is for innovative education strategies, towards greater efficiency and effectiveness in the delivery of educational services.

We strongly believe that the vision of access to quality education also means equality of educational opportunity for both the rich as well as for the poorer sections of our communities. Access to quality education means that everyone should have the opportunity not only to enter a given educational institution, whether public or private, or have access to a given form of training or retraining, but also to be given the opportunity to complete their education and have prospects of obtaining better options in life. The concern for "Access to Quality Education, Excellence in Educational Services" is a response to the age-old educational reality that equality of access does not guarantee equality of success, equality of opportunity does not ensure equality of results.

This reality is all too obvious if we look at the vastly different chances of school survival of poor children from disadvantaged sections of society compared to their well-to-do, upper-class cousins, the children of the rich. Yes, it will be seen that there is a rather fair representation of all income groups at the primary level, but as one proceeds to the secondary and higher education levels, there are fewer and fewer children from the bottom third while those from the top third are increasingly dominating the scene. At the college or university level, there are even fewer poor students while the rich are grossly over-represented. And for as long as inequality of educational results or achievements persists, inequalities of income, class and status will also persist. This is the vicious cycle of low economic status causing early failure in school or increase in school dropouts, and low educational attainments leading to unskilled, low-income employment and low social status.

How then must we respond to this age-old reality of school leavers/dropouts, the educated unemployed, and the illiterates?

If the educational sector is to serve as a successful agent of cultural, social and economic development, education must go beyond the traditional formal structure of schools and must necessarily include all forms of schooling where teaching-learning occurs. Educational planners, policy makers, and administrators must no longer be content with the traditional delivery of learning services. Neither should the content of education be regarded as static, standard and uniform. Educators must think of serving not only the limited number of persons in school but also those outside, especially because the latter constitute a sizable clientele that calls for immediate attention.

To be relevant means to continuously develop curricula to meet the learning needs of each type of learner. Today, the types of learners have become varied and complex. The question of "quality" and "relevance" calls for giving more attention to ways and means of effectively delivering the relevant content in an appropriate form to the right clientele. Being relevant means adapting educational services to local needs. Community-based education implies the need to introduce the concept of flexibility and diversity in the system, adapting it to the needs of the local population and developing approaches relevant to local life and culture. This is particularly true when there are cultural barriers to learning, which may be the case with ethnic and cultural minorities who do not identify with the objectives and content of the educational program. In this case, the curriculum may have to be modified and complemented with materials relevant to local culture and traditions. Relevance is also enhanced when educators take into account community needs for knowledge as well as skills for improving health welfare and living conditions. The important issue to be considered thenthat of combining local relevance of the curriculum with a common core of learning needs.

THE WED PROJECT

The Notre Dame Foundation for Charitable Activities, Inc. - Women In Enterprise Development (NDFCAI-WED) was accredited by the United States Agency for International

Development as a PVO in 1987 to serve the socio-economic needs of the indigents in the Archdiocese of Cotabato. Because it is also at the forefront of the advocacy, promotion, and implementation of non-formal education projects in Muslim Mindanao, the Philippines, the Foundation also has the formidable task of sustaining literacy and providing entrepreneurial skills among Muslim, Christian and Lumad (indigenous peoples) learners so that they can become economically self-reliant. The Foundation believes that neo-literates are threatened by regression to illiteracy when not properly trained for self-productivity. Thus, in its various projects, emphasis is given to enterprise development, i.e., skills training, micro-lending, and technical assistance in cooperative formation, to ensure that learners are armed with the necessary competence for establishing small family enterprises that can uplift their living standards.

Today, after having graduated hundreds of women from the literacy and entrepreneurial skills training courses, WED continues to keep a long list of applicants, including *imams* and *ustadzes*. Moreover, WED training centers are built on land donated by the community members, who also offer free labor. With financial support from different international and local organizations, WED has been able to replicate its project in the municipalities of the Autonomous Region of Muslim Mindanao. It is highly respected, credible and fully accepted as a non-government organization (NGO) engaged in literacy and enterprise development work. In fact, in the Philippines it is considered a model literacy program implementor. The project has recieved numerous awards, including the 1995 Outstanding National Literacy Program for Philippines sponsored by the UNESCO Philippine National Commission, the Department of Education, Culture and Sports (DECS) and the Rotary Club of Manila; the 1996 Philippine Best Projects for Community Development sponsored by the Commission on Population (POPCOM); and the prestigious 1997 UNESCO King Sejong International Literacy Prize sponsored by the UNESCO Headquarters in Paris and the Government of the Republic of Korea. Recently, it was awarded the 1998 Rafael M. Salas Population and Development Award (individual and institution categories) for its outstanding achievement and support in the field of population and development.

DEVELOPMENT PHILOSOPHY

The Foundation envisions the empowerment of women with skills, knowledge, and training to enable them to develop and gain control over their lives.

It hopes to help women become active participants in the mainstream of economic activity. Through adult education/functional literacy, it aims to develop entrepreneurship; increase the productivity, income and managerial capabilities of the beneficiaries; and promote and improve health and nutrition habits and civic consciousness.

Development Content

The NDFCAI-WED program is a ladderized type of adult learning continuing education. No applicant has ever been declined because of illiteracy. Equal opportunity is afforded to everyone wanting to grow and become productive, regardless of her religion, race or creed.

Located in a pluralistic society, the NDFCAI-WED program is a vehicle for the promotion of peace and intra-faith understanding. Its lessons focus on the development of the total person, based on respect for and promotion of life and human rights, truth, justice and peace. Respect for personhood is its guiding principle.

Classes are opened after the need for these has been determined via a baseline community survey and in consultation with the local government and *barangay* leaders. Well-known Muslim leaders are often tapped as resource persons.

The NDFCAI-WED offers seven programs, that have transformed hundreds of women and out-of-school youth from being dependent, unproductive individuals to self-confident, productive, and economically independent individuals. These are:

    a. Functional Literacy/Adult Education
    b. Skills and Entrepreneurship Development Trainings
    c. Micro-credit Assistance
    d. Marketing Assistance
    e. Cooperative Formation and Development Assistance
    f. Technical Assistance and Consultancy
    g. Research and Advocacy

WED's Seven Programs

Functional Literacy/Adult Education

Unemployed illiterate women living in depressed areas who want to be more productive can participate in the NDFCAI-WED program by enrolling for one year in its Functional Literacy/Adult Education center in the local communities. These centers are built through "self-help" voluntary labor of the families and act as "feeder" classes for the skills and entrepreneurship training.

Classes in this program are classified into two levels:

    1) Basic Adult Education (BAED. This is designed to provide basic non-formal education on the three R's (reading, writing and numeracy) using Filipino as medium of instruction. Integrated in the learning

curriculum are community and social issues/topics such as health and hygiene, civic consciousness, environmental sanitation, protection and conservation, responsible parenthood, gender and development, peace and development, and entrepreneurship.

2) Advanced Adult Education (ADED). BAED graduates who are interested in continuing their education may enrol in this class. English instruction is now a part of the module and BAED topics are used for advanced literacy education. This class also targets the school leavers/dropouts who are literate in Filipino but illiterate in English.

It is noteworthy that most of the learners have developed proprietary feelings towards the project and are assisting the facilitators by serving as mentors.

ENTREPRENEURSHIP DEVELOPMENT AND SKILLS TRAINING:

Upon graduation from the functional literacy classes, and if the learner shows high numeracy and literacy proficiency, she will be encouraged to enroll in a five-month skills training course in garments, handicrafts, or food production. The course is also open to indigent/ needy applicants of Cotabato City and surrounding areas.

With grants from the USAID, the project graduated more than 1,200 Muslim and Christian beneficiaries in 1996. At present, with the assistance of the Asian Development Bank, the Aboitiz Group Foundation, Inc., and the Provincial Government of Maguindanao (the local funding agencies), the project aims to directly benefit more than 1,000 clients. The project also keeps a long waitlist of would-be participants.

This NDFCAI-WED project component has two levels:

1) Basic Skills and Entrepreneurship Training (BEST). This is designed for those without any background in garments-making or food processing and small business management and has a duration of three to five months. The trainees are exposed to special learning exercises that aim to build self-awareness and self-confidence. Social responsibility, value formation, spiritual development, personal health and hygiene, business management, entrepreneurship, production plan, marketing, credit responsibilities, taxes and licensing, bookkeeping, etc. are included in the lessons.

2) Advanced Skills and Entrepreneurship Training (ASET). These are short-term courses designed to provide BEST graduates and other entrepreneurs with advanced and specialized skills. There are classes on garments, handicrafts, food processing, entrepreneurial management, and making flower arrangements, corsages, headbands, stuffed toys, and other souvenir items.

The project's success in the communities being served can be attributed to the community organizing work conducted beforehand. Support is generated through consultations with the local officials. Social mobilization, such as house-to-house surveys and barangay meetings, are also conducted.

At present, there are two kinds of training courses based on location: 1) the center-based skills training, and 2) the barangay or community-based skills training. In the first scheme, learners go to the identified training centers for skills classes. The second scheme requires WED staff and trainers to go to identified communities for the training courses. For the barangay or community-based training, the project conceptualized the mobile training program, which has the following features:

1) trainings are localized;

2) will respond to requests from communities to conduct demonstrations and crash courses on specific projects;

3) participants acquire skills and avail of new technology in a short time;

4) utilizes the natural and human resources in the area;

5) coordinates with concerned local government agencies for new methodologies, market and resource persons;

6) utilizes the Foundation's vehicle to transport equipment and training materials from one community to another; and

7) can be conducted in any conducive area (a beneficiary's house or backyard, a *barangay* hall or health center, unoccupied rooms of the home for the aged, a local parish church meeting room, etc.).

The mobile training strategy was employed to help poor but interested women in depressed and hard-to-reach communities to attend the training program with the least transportation costs, as well as to assist more areas at the shortest possible time.

The approaches used are personalized instruction, demonstration and return demonstrations, workshops, hands-on training, lectures, quizzes, and group discussions. The participants are exposed to special learning exercises to build skills in garments and handicrafts, micro-business management, and social and credit responsibility.

CREDIT ASSISTANCE PROGRAM

This is designed to provide seed capital for the skills training graduates who are willing to put up home-based businesses and who show business management potentials. The program also extends credit assistance to existing micro-entrepreneurs.

Financial assistance is given following certain criteria. One of these is the applicant's entrepreneurial potential. Clarity and soundness of business plan is also considered. If loan beneficiaries prove to be good borrowers, succeeding loans can be availed of with increased ceilings. Market promotion activities are likewise undertaken with the beneficiaries.

MARKETING ASSISTANCE

The WED Crafts Center serves as a marketing center for the products of WED beneficiaries and other entrepreneurs. Products are displayed and sold on consignment basis. The Center also links interested buyers with the entrepreneurs. Technical assistance is provided in the marketing, design and packaging of products. Referrals are also made to potential buyers within and outside the city.

CO-OPERATIVE FORMATION ASSISTANCE

WED has assisted in the formation of two multi-purpose co-operatives composed of its graduates and other entrepreneurs: the Market Vendors Multi-purpose Co-operative and the WED Cotabato KrIslam Multi-purpose Co-operative. They provide micro-lending, savings deposit generation, bulk-buying and marketing of projects, and raw materials purchasing services to their members.

AS of 1997, the co-operatives have more than 200 members and an accumulated net revenue of more than one million pesos.

TECHNICAL ASSISTANCE & CONSULTANCY

Through the years, the NDFCAI-WED has made a name for itself in the area of providing technical assistance and consultancy services to various co-operatives, non-government organizations, and local government units operating in the Autonomous Region in Muslim Mindanao.

Its capability-building services focus on Community-based Strategic Planning and Management, Organizational Formation and Development, Project Development using the community development model, Financial Management, Leadership, Management and Supervision, Marketing Management, Production Management, Co-operative Formation and Development Operations Management, Management of Change, Micro-economics, Resource Generation Participatory Action Research/Participatory Rapid Assessment, Gender and Development, Planning, Implementing, Monitoring and Evaluation, Peace Culture and Peace-building, Instructional Materials Development, Facilitator/Staff Development, Trainors' Training, Team-building and Conflict Resolution, Project Coordination, Community Organizing, Local Governance, Technology of Participation, and the Community-based Enterprise System.

Its consultancy experience focuses on Community-based Enterprise System, Literacy and Non-formal Education, Small and Medium Enterprise Development, and Gender and Equity/Women and Development

Research and Advocacy

The Foundation has also conducted various researches and surveys in the field of women and development, group formation, economics, education and training. It is also into networking, linkaging, and advocacy.

The project's success in its enterprise development endeavors may be attributed to:

a. the strong collaboration with the local government units and the support of community leaders in the areas being served. This can be seen in their willingness to provide training venues, chairs, and other necessary facilities and human support for the training.

b. the strong coordination with other government line agencies, particularly those with existing community training programs.

c. the strong interest of the community to learn and earn.

d. the presence of a contact person and/ or facilitator-organizer in the area.

e. the implementation of new strategies for training packages that are community- and culture-sensitive;

f. and dedicated staff, trainors and facilitators.

Community Participation in Monitoring and Evaluation of WED Project Activities

Monitoring and Evaluation (M&E) are an integral part of any development project/program initiative because they constitute a response mechanism to identify the strengths, weakness, and possible gaps between planned and actual activities; to make appropriate decisions on operations and strategies employed at various levels or stages of project/program implementation; and to determine whether the organization is reaching its intended beneficiaries. M&E is intended to improve and develop the service delivery and operation of a program.

Working together is a key element in M&E. Community members, local leaders, and other stakeholders get involved in the process of developing M&E approaches, and together find ways of solving gaps, issues, and problems, while highlighting the project's successes.

Monitoring and Evaluation: The Concept

Monitoring and Evaluation Concepts

Monitoring and Evaluation are often used interchangeably and synonymously. But these two ideas are considered different components that interface only in time frame.

Monitoring efforts aim to ensure that the project/program is properly implemented. It only aims to provide profiles of activities at the implementation level. Monitoring work commences simultaneously with the start of the program.

Evaluation, on the other hand, aims to examine the project in its entirety—the concept, inputs, process and outputs, as well as outcome—and make recommendations that may lead to the revision of the program design or its replacement. It aims to examine experiences to verify whether stated objectives were accomplished, how and why these objectives were accomplished, as well as how and why these objectives were or were not accomplished. It may also recommend changes on the program's future courses of action. Evaluation work is undertaken at regular intervals sometime after the project/program implementation has started.

The basic difference between Monitoring and Evaluation lies in their purposes. The major purpose of monitoring is to improve and perfect the implementation of the program while the purpose of evaluation is to assess and judge its performance.

Thus, monitoring is defined as a system that follows a well-designed process of collecting and analyzing information of all events with the view of improving project/program implementation.

Evaluation is defined as a systematic process of collecting and analyzing data in order to determine the relevance, effectiveness, and impact of activities in the light of their objectives.

The Importance and Benefits of Monitoring and Evaluation

Monitoring and Evaluation are important phases of any project implementation because:
- It serves as basis for modifying or revising ongoing projects/programs. Sufficient information for putting interventions in place is critical to the success of a program.

- It can provide a basis for planning and strategy formulation in the succeeding phases of the project/program.
- It is a necessary component in the preparation and conduct of impact assessment.
- Who are deriving benefits from the program? How is the delivery of services being done? These are some questions that can be answered only if there is a monitoring system in place.
- It allows for the measurement of project implementation against project plans and budget allocations.
- It can identify implementation problems, weaknesses, gaps, bottleneck areas, issues, threats, and potential sources of delay. Thus, corrective action may be taken.
- It can identify success stories, experiences, and strategies and utilize the insights gained in planning the subsequent activities of the project/program.
- It can provide comparative analysis, along financial cost and physical implementation, with similar ongoing projects.

WED'S ACTUAL MONITORING AND EVALUATION PRACTICES

WED monitoring and evaluation practices utilize the gender-based participatory approach where the community, the Foundation, and project stakeholders together plan and decide how to improve the organisation for it to effectively provide services.

Monitoring, follow-up, and evaluation of WED activities are undertaken regularly to ensure effective project implementation. Such a policy serves dual functions. First, should an error or problem occur, appropriate corrections could be instituted immediately. Second, the internal evaluation at any given point helps project management in decision-making and facilitates immediate action.

MONITORING AND EVALUATION STRUCTURE: WHO ARE INVOLVED?

In monitoring and evaluation, the Foundation works with and involves the following groups in order to come up with sufficient information to ensure an effective and efficient literacy program:

- Learners: the beneficiaries of the project who are marginalised women and girls, out-of-school youth, and the unemployed

- Community: traditional leaders, local government units, contact persons, key informants, and community members
- Implementing Agency: the Notre Dame Foundation for Charitable Activities, Inc.-Women in Enterprise Development, particularly the facilitators, project coordinators, monitoring and evaluation officer, finance officer, and executive director
- Other Stakeholders: these include the national government line agencies, other literacy implementors, donor agencies, and other institutions that have a stake in the project

WED uses a collaborative approach that encourages a more active role for the community. A series of consultations and dialogues are undertaken to generate local support. Detailed information is given about the project and how it can help community members improve their lives. The community helps the project identify where the illiterates are and encourage them to join the literacy classes. They provide valuable inputs about the socio-political dynamics in one area. They also help select the venue where the literacy classes will be held, and determine the schedule of classes.

The collaborative approach used by WED involves the learners in identifying and developing learning objectives, monitoring and evaluation indicators, techniques and criteria incorporating the objectives, and indicators of competency required by the DECS-Bureau of Non-Formal Education. Group decision-making, learning contracts, and grading contracts are set up to be the basis of monitoring and evaluation. The approach is based on the belief that adults have not only a right but also a responsibility to take an active role in determining all phases of their learning experiences.

The information collected at the local level are used by top management to present a clear and objective situation of the community and the progress achieved by the project, which in turn can help the decision makers and donor agencies in decision making.

MONITORING AND EVALUATION PROCESS: WHAT TO COLLECT AND HOW TO ANALYZE MONITORING DATA AND INFORMATION

- **Monitoring and Evaluation of Learners**

In the literacy class, the WED facilitator monitors the performance and learning achievement of the learners using various monitoring tools. The registration forms are used to determine their literacy level; the attendance record is used to determine their participation in the literacy class as well as determine the level of their writing skills; tests, assignments and individual learners portfolio all determine progress. The learners are evaluated based on their reading and comprehension skills, writing skills, numeracy skills, and community participation skills.

The learner also participates in monitoring and evaluating their literacy progress by answering the Self-Assessment Progress Review (SAPR) form.

The project staff, consisting of the project coordinator, the monitoring officer, and the director, periodically visit the literacy class to determine the progress of the learners and validate the reports provided by the facilitator and the community members. Techniques such as observation, interview, group discussion, meetings, documentation and actual demonstration, as well as tools such as monitoring checklists, are used to generate and validate information at the class level.

The community members, who are the "silent eyes and ears" of the community, also voluntarily monitor the progress of the learners. They can provide appropriate support for the learners, as well as make recommendations to the project.

- Monitoring and Evaluation of the Facilitator

The learners also evaluate the performance of the facilitator with the use of the Facilitator Performance Evaluation. The learners evaluate the dedication, commitment and effectiveness of the facilitator in conducting the literacy class. If the learners are not satisfied with their current facilitator, they do not hesitate to ask the project coordinators and local contact persons to replace him/her.

The project staff also monitor the performance and effectiveness of the facilitator. They focus on whether the learning and facilitating techniques, strategies and methodologies used by the facilitator are appropriate for the learners' level, and whether the facilitator follows the basic curriculum for non-formal education.

The community also monitors the performance and attendance of the facilitators. Frequent absences of the facilitator result in a warning, suspension, and eventually termination from work.

- LEARNING ACTIVITIES/CLASS

The learners, the facilitator and the community assist the project staff in monitoring learning activities. One consideration is whether the activities undertaken are expressive of the learner's individual needs/community needs and whether they facilitate the learning process. The monitoring focuses on the adequacy of teaching and learning materials available at the community. The learners are encouraged to evaluate the class activities. The following questions are often asked: Are the learners actively participating in discussions? Are the schedules being followed? What is the duration of one learning session? Is the prescribed curriculum being used? How many males and females attend the literacy class? Do learners initiate community activities or are they involved in community activities? Usually, various M&E tools are used to elicit answers to these questions, including interviews, observation, and institutional monitoring checklists.

The M&E team collects and analyses the following:

- Learner's profile
- Facilitator's profile
- Learner's progress and skills acquired
- Facilitator's effectiveness and competency
- Community involvement, participation, local resource mobilization and support
- Sufficiency, appropriateness, and usefulness of learning materials and teaching aids
- Relevance of the curriculum used
- Types of supervision support provided
- Physical facilities and learning centers
- Institutional capability to manage the literacy project
- Problems and highlights of project implementation
- Impact of project implementation
- Adequacy of budget
- Fund management
- Sustainability

Monitoring and Evaluation Phases: When to Monitor and Evaluate

Each of the four major phases of the literacy project implementation is monitored and evaluated.

• Pre-Implementation Phase

During the planning and development of the literacy project, an M&E mechanism is set up using qualitative, quantitative, participative, equity, and gender-based indicators to determine the quality of the services to be provided. Specifically, the main tasks of M&E

at this stage are: 1) to monitor and review whether the plan and materials developed are synchronized with the schedule, staff activities, and strategies to be used; 2) to assess whether the institution has systems, resources, and technical experience to successfully implement a project for a certain period; and 3) to review the implementation plan or determine activities for implementation. The M&E questions include: Does the implementor have sound guidelines for the operation of a particular activity? Are there innovations to assure successful implementation and avoid a repetition of the mistakes committed in the past? Has the service provider undertaken the necessary social mobilization? Is the service provider a trusted entity in the community? Are the people confident about participating in the learning classes?

Needs assessment, baseline surveys, and rapid assessments are usually conducted by WED at this phase of the project.

- Implementation Phase

At this stage, the main task of M&E is to collect evidence about the effectiveness of the program and services under various conditions. Ongoing M&E is an essential part of the management information system and takes place at intervals during the implementation of the project. The primary focus of M&E is usually the process of implementation. The findings and recommendations are meant to assist in resolving immediate problems. Progress reports, accomplishment reports, institutional monitoring, process evaluation, and learner and facilitator evaluation are conducted at this stage. M&E at this stage is a mechanism by which the managers can take preventive or corrective actions to keep the project on course.

- Completion Phase

During the completion stage, M&E is conducted to present the overall outputs, results, effects, and impact of literacy implementation. Terminal reports, summary evaluations, and impact assessments are usually made.

Terminal evaluation is the analysis of the project at the end of its life in order to determine its relevance, effectiveness, and likely impact. It will normally be undertaken by an evaluation team external to the project. Terminal evaluations often have to consider the results of the project (just like ongoing evaluation) as well as provide the basis for decisions about future actions. The findings and recommendations of terminal evaluations are frequently used when an extension of the project is considered, including any alterations in design and use of resources. They can also be useful in deriving lessons for similar projects.

- **Ex-post Implementation Phase**

    M&E takes place after project completion and goes into greater depth than ongoing and terminal monitoring and evaluation. The focus is on the analysis of impact. A thorough examination of the outputs produced and the effects generated is required because without an in-depth analysis of both, it is not feasible to trace the actual or potential impact of the project.

    Ex-post M&E provides feedback lessons for the future in terms of policies, design, institutional framework, implementation strategy, and the role played by complementary factors in generating effects and impact.

FEEDBACK FROM MONITORING AND EVALUATION: WHO, WHEN AND IN WHICH FORM TO REPORT

It is evident that evaluation is undertaken not only to assess the performance and achievements of projects in terms of their relevance, efficiency, and effectiveness, but also to enable managers, planners, and policy makers to learn lessons for the improvement of both existing and new projects. This is known as feedback and evaluation. A project without feedback is a waste of effort and resources. To be effective, however, feedback must satisfy several levels in the decision-making hierarchy.

In promoting and strengthening feedback, it is important to recognize that:

- M&E must be properly substantiated with a need to focus on specific issues and not on insignificant points or personality problems.
- A feedback mechanism needs to be established by policy makers and top management. Thus, the M&E team must work closely with them.
- Reliance on feedback should be based on formal arrangements (official reporting) as well as informal arrangements (seminars).
- Findings and lessons gained for feedback need to be tactfully packaged when disseminated in order to improve receptiveness of the managers.

CONCLUSION

Monitoring and evaluation can be a powerful tool for the institutionalization and mainstreaming of a participatory and gendered approach to successful project management and implementation. M&E provides timely and periodic feedback and identifies problem areas that require solutions and immediate action, thus helping the project save precious time and money.

M&E is continuously conducted during the entire duration of project implementation. However, not all indicators are applicable at all phases and levels of the project. It is up to the learners, community, service providers, and donor agencies to come up with a common or required indicator applicable at a certain level or phase. It is at this point that we should develop and innovate techniques and strategies for monitoring and evaluating projects successfully. Those of us who hold strategic positions within our given institutions have the capacity and influence to mainstream and integrate gender and development concerns within our programs and projects.

Mainstreaming gender has never been a problem for the Women in Enterprise Development basically because it is a gender-responsive project. It was designed as early as 1984 in response to the sad plight of women and girls in our communities. It is our vision and mission to continuously advocate and work for the full integration of women in the development process. And this is a mandate we intend to pursue.

PART 2
Going Beyond Quantitative Measures

An Evaluation of the Victoria Mxenge Housing Development Association from a Gender Perspective

Salma Ismail

This article was written in an attempt to understand the active role of women in housing projects. Focusing on the Victoria Mxenge Housing Development Association (VMHDA) in Cape Town, it describes how women, guided by their social vision, have successfully organised in an often hostile urban environment.

HISTORICAL OVERVIEW

South Africa's history has been characterised by waves of land hunger, dispossession (Land Act of 1913 and 1936), forced removals, and the growth of informal settlements. Forced removals and the Group Areas Act of 1966 were strategies employed in the cities to wage war against black people; these gave the government licence not to provide housing and other social services to the poor. The lack of housing must therefore be seen in the context of these policies which created poverty, inequity, and a host of other sociopolitical and spatial problems. The rapid growth in population and unemployment and the economic recession have exacerbated the problem of lack of housing. For example, in the Western Cape, it is estimated that there is a backlog of 114,000 houses.

Against the backdrop of huge housing backlogs and the new government's problems with delivery of housing services, members of the VMHDA have successfully pooled their resources and realised their dreams of financing, building, and owning their own homes.

The VMHDA is a housing savings programme that is an affiliate of the South African Homeless People's Federation[1] which was established in 1994. The VMHDA is situated off Lansdowne Road, in Philippi, in Cape Town, on the way to Guguletu opposite the Ikapa Town Council. When the project started, there were only eight members, all women.

One of the founding members, Patricia Matolengwe, went to a meeting organised by the People's Dialogue[2] in January 1992. On her return, she and other members of the African National Congress Women's League (ANCWL) started the housing scheme along the lines laid out by the People's Dialogue. They named the housing scheme in honor of Victoria Mxenge, a Durban-based political activist and human right's lawyer who was assassinated on August 5, 1985.

Many of the women who became members of the VMHDA are members of the ANCWL. They first heard about the plans for a housing savings group during ANCWL meetings. Rose Maso joined the VMHDA in 1992. She recalls the initial mobilisation:

> This project was brought by Patricia Matolengwe, she brought it to the women who were meeting time and again to discuss how they can move out of the shacks.

According to the People's Dialogue (June 1994:1):

> Not one of them could have imagined that the little cooperative which they had formed was soon to become one of the strongest people-based housing organisations in South Africa. In May 1992, VM was the youngest and smallest savings collective in the People's Dialogue Federation of Housing Savings Scheme. Today they are the benchmark against which all other groups measure progress.

The VMHDA project was one of 13 applicants for Catholic Church-owned land in Philippi. The Catholic Church wanted to make the land available to the community. In the initial discussions about the land, the women had problems participating effectively in forums. However, encouraged by the experiences of women in India and Latin America, the women of VM learned strategies to overcome the lack of political experience. They went to meetings with children on their backs, spoke in Xhosa, and used role playing and singing to build their confidence. The women designed and conducted their own survey, listing their employment details, housing details, household information, migratory histories, and housing savings record. This information was put together in a document titled "What we need now is the land", and circulated. Within two months, the title to the land was transferred to the VMHDA.

The women believe that they were rightfully given the land. They not only lived there; they had also demonstrated their need and ability to save money and build houses (People's Dialogue, September 1994:5).

I came to know of the project through Patricia Matolengwe, who was a student in my course at the Centre for Adult and Continuing Education. Since then I have been talking to the women informally and formally over many months, I would like the voices of the women to be heard above those of secondary sources.

WOMEN INVOLVED IN HOUSING

When I first came to Victoria Mxenge in 1994, the women were learning to make bricks with Mama Mzisa's help, to lay foundations, and to make models of their dream homes. With each visit, I encountered a new development. In 1995, the first houses were built. In 1996, the women were unable to build in Victoria Mxenge because the land was being prepared for the infrastructure, including electricity cables and sanitation pipes. At this time, they helped their sister organisation in Maccassar and built 61 houses there. In February 1997, construction of the streets began. When I returned in April 1997, the streets had been completed and named after Patricia Matolengwe and Sanki Mthembi-Nkondo (Minister of Housing). There was one male name, that of Shaun Cuff from the People's Dialogue. Then, the VMHDA began building the community centre, the day-care centre, and more houses.

These new developments both inspired and bewildered me. So I began asking questions: Why are women involved in housing? What makes them persevere, given that the process is so slow and fraught with obstacles? What is it that makes the women of Victoria Mxenge (VM) so special? Is it their gender, their rural origins, their histories of dispossession, their hopes for the future, their children, the present political climate that holds out opportunities to rebuild their lives?

To the first question, the women give a simple answer:

> We dream of houses and therefore we must build them.

Patricia says:

> What motivates the women [is] the need for a house, the dynamism of working with other women, and the strong, supportive relationships that have been formed.

> The women share the experience of coming from rural areas, living in squatter settlements, being labeled illegal, being subjected to forced removals, living without social services and often without husbands. Sharing common origins and vulnerabilities, they are willing to find solutions to their problems through discussion. (Ismail, 1996:4).

The second reason that is given is that they build on the gender roles which function in rural areas, which they understand well. In the rural areas, it is the women who build the homes and maintain the household. Mama Rosa says:

> We were not born in Cape Town. We are from the Transkei. Women from the rural areas are strong and used to standing up and planning on their own for their household.

This view is well-documented by Dankelman and Davidson (1987:5). Writing on women in rural Africa, they say:

> Women are bound together by the common fact of their tremendous work burden; they attend to all the survival tasks of growing food, fetching water and fuel, looking after the children and generally sustaining family life.

Caroline White's (1993) research on women who have left the rural areas to live in Johannesburg supports this description of African women's experience. Women living in the city carry a double load of wage employment and household tasks and child care in which their partners take no or a minimal share.

The women do not mind voluntary work if they know it will improve their lives and their children's future. All the women I spoke to said that on arrival from the rural areas they had found employment as domestic workers, even though some of them have passed standard eight or nine. The women attribute this to not being fluent in English and not having marketable skills. The fact that they all have madams and share common forms of abuse in this kind of employment is another bonding mechanism.

The women of the VMHDA see themselves as protectors of the family and community. In their songs, they sing of women as mothers of the nation. Under apartheid, the family's existence was always under threat. Thus, they feel that their first responsibility is restoring relations within the family and community. Hence, the VMHDA slogan: "We are not only building houses; we are building people and a community."

ORGANIZING WOMEN

Of the 286 VMHDA members, only five are men. Xoliswa and Veliswa say that men are not discouraged from joining:

> We are not against men being part of us. But we want the majority to be women. We are the ones who feel the pain of looking after the children and having to witness our houses burning and the rain coming inside the house. Even when it comes to evictions the women are at the forefront protecting the houses.

Mama Msiza and Nonkangelani add. "Men earn salaries. Our salaries are our houses. It is clear to us that we are very important in the family even if the man calls us the tail end of the family...because we are the ones who know how to spend the money for food, clothes and paraffin even if the money is very little."

Patricia says the men do help during public holidays and when on leave.[3]

But generally, their views on men are not very complimentary. Many say they have lost their husbands to girlfriends, shebeens (drinking houses), the hostels which some men refuse to vacate. They also disapprove of the men's propensity to resolve conflict by fighting. Mama Mzisa says men like to fight and she points to the taxi conflict as an example of a man's organisation. In contrast, she says, "that in Kwazulu-Natal, the women from all the different political parties, work together. This reinforces the women's belief that they have to be in the majority in the Homeless People's Federation."

Tata Sigebe, one of the few male members of the VMHDA, comes to the men's defence. He says, "The men are away at work all day. They leave early and come home late. They have very little time."

The women do not see their organisation as threatening to men, yet their activism has been of concern to the men, as it seems to threaten the delicate power balance of relationships. On the one hand, the men know in their hearts who built the houses. They realise that their wives are skilled and knowledgeable. On the other hand, this creates a tacit understanding that relationships, the expectations, and the demands made of each other have changed. The women say they judge men differently; they want fairness and respect; and they value the men for their ability to keep the family together. For single parents, it is the community that provides their main support system.

Cross and Friedman's (1997:23) research supports the women's opinions. They conclude that as a result of a breakdown of old values (patriarchal law) in the city and especially in the rural areas, when there is a reliance on wages, "women may find themselves struggling alone, with fewer resources and less support from their husbands, sons and male relatives."

LAND, HOUSING AND SUBSIDIES

The legal position of South African women in relation to land and home ownership has gone through dramatic changes under the new Constitution of 1996. Women may own land and houses and a special provision has been made to protect the rights of women such as the Equality Clause (1996) which does away with discriminatory practices. The new Housing Act (1997: 6) promotes single and joint ownership of houses. It contains clauses which prohibit unfair practices on the grounds of gender and makes specific reference to the housing needs of marginalised women, the cultural identity of different groups which may lead to diversity in housing demands, as well as the critical need for housing development in rural and urban areas.

However, in the former homelands, the new laws are not yet operative. The power of traditional authorities remains largely unquestioned. People are ignorant of the new laws and the social perception of ownership as a male preserve is not necessarily challenged when the administrators of the law are blind to the changes. The communal tenure system (whereby the Chief distributes land to male heads of households) and customary inheritance laws are still applied. Under these laws women cannot own, hold rights to, or inherit land from their husbands.

While the Equality Clause in the new Constitution of 1996 has formally brought an end to this discriminatory situation on paper, the subordinate position of women with regard to land rights has not changed radically. As a consequence, women can and do become homeless when their marriages break down or their husbands die.

In the urban context, the state previously allocated housing to male heads of households. But under the new Housing Act (1997:8), women who are financially secure, including women involved in saving clubs and who are building their own homes, have the choice of ownership. Under the laws governing housing subsidies, married and unmarried couples, single women and men over the age of 21 with dependents, and pensioners with dependents can apply for subsidies. The amount of subsidy (which ranges from R10,000 to R15,000) depends on the household's income. Where land development costs are high, a 15 percent supplement may be applied for. The applicant/home owner can apply for joint ownership.

However, social perceptions of land and home ownership have not always operated in women's favour. Often, even when the woman is the applicant, her partner will claim ownership. Although the laws appear to be gender-neutral, social practices and perceptions are more slow to change.

Building on rural strengths

Their common identity in a hostile urban environment is the fertile ground on which the VMHDA has planted the dream of a secure home for families and a form of communal living that is protective and rewarding for them on many levels.

What makes the VMHDA women different from most women in the urban areas who do not build their own homes, is that they feel a common identity. Most of them came from the former Transkei and Ciskei. They have suffered constant removals, first at the hands of the apartheid state, then vigilante groups, and now criminal elements who threaten their new homes. They have formed a network of supportive relationships that fill in for those in the rural community they have come from.

For the women who have joined the VMHDA, being rural depends more on where one was born than on where one lives. Rural links arising from membership in family clans, churches, and different villages bring people to Victoria Mxenge. Families find relatives and friends through these networks, as well as information about where to live and work in the city. The identity of rural or urban is the result not of geographical space but of belief systems that help to forge identities. The values on which one is raised, the social roles and relationships that were fostered, the clothes one wears, the form that celebrations take—these make up one's identity.

Some in the urban community view them as potential criminals and competition for resources like land and subsidies for housing. But Patricia points out that people in the rural areas are imbued with the philosophy and practice of sharing and discussing experiences and finding solutions to problems. In rural areas, an oral culture prevails. This makes it easier to sit down and talk. Through the Homeless Peoples Federation, the women of the VMHDA have come in contact with different people who have named this part of their tradition as ubuntu, which means dialogue and participatory democracy. They take pride in the fact that people from other countries, such as India (most notably Mahila Milan) and Brazil (Cearah Periferia),[4] value this practice. They have learned from these networks and strengthened their confidence in dialogue. They talk about their problems, care for each other's children, work together as a team. Their main conflict resolution skill is to talk about problems and find joint solutions. And they are concerned with whether an activity or project benefits each individual and builds each person's confidence.

COMMUNAL VALUES

The women do not romanticise the traditions of communal living but emphasise that this is a way of ensuring their survival. They point out that poor people need to stick together, as only they will support one another. They say that individual households do not have the stamina or skills required to deal with the complicated procedures of securing land tenure, applying for housing subsidies, or building their own homes. In times of rising inflation, banding together is one way of ensuring that people will have water, sanitation, and electricity, and be able to continue paying for these necessities. As poor people they would never be able to sustain this development on their own. They say, "The savings scheme is not so much about collecting money as it is about collecting people. Saving is the glue that helps people to stick together."

Xoliswa, who manages the daily savings of the group, describes the underlying community development processes that go with saving.

> The daily collectors are like social workers. Everyday they go to the houses and they see the situation of each house. Then we hear if someone is sick or if there is no food in someone's house. If it is someone who is active in our organisation, then we decide to give her money. We do not focus on money but [on whether] that person is someone we trust and [one who] is active.

The customary law of communal ownership of the land has made it easier to form a housing association. The land is owned communally, undercutting potential conflict between husbands and wives. However, households do have the option of buying out their share. Also, the woman has the option of owning the house as she takes out the loan in her name. This is put forward as an option because perceptions of land rights and home ownership are still very much rooted in the social values of the traditional land tenure system. The women generally agree that the house should be in their name. However, many fear a breakdown of their marriage or less financial support from their husbands if they choose ownership of the house. In these cases, the houses are jointly owned by the couple.

Cross and Friedman's (1997:24) research in rural areas confirms the view that, "an increase in women's greater access to resources appears to result in men's unwillingness to support women financially."

Following customary practice, the VMHDA Land Committee allocates the land to members. Each household gets the same size plot. Veliswa, who sits on this committee, sometimes has to deal with difficult issues:

I have learned to talk to people and remain calm, as it is not easy to allocate plots and to show someone a piece of land that has nothing on it. Sometimes two people want the same plot. In these cases, the committee resolves the problem.

STRATEGIES AND TACTICS

The biggest challenges facing the VMHDA are obtaining secure land tenure so they can build their houses, and negotiating financing for building houses and infrastructure.

The strategies used to obtain these resources are found within the VMHDA philosophy and organisational structure. The democratic participatory structure of the organisation provides the framework for a cohesive set of relationships. At the same time, emphasis is placed on each individual's part in the process, from saving to building and negotiating for land and housing finance. Everyone is a leader in these processes. They are learning continuously, in spite of their low levels of formal literacy, by observation and by doing, and from each other rather than from the experts.

Skeptical of the kinds of training received from experts, the women say they prefer to learn from people in a similar predicament. They use a number of organisational strategies, including workshops, role play, concerts, songs and poetry, to recruit new members, inform members of new developments, illustrate to new members how the saving schemes function, express criticisms of the government, and celebrate achievements. When they want to increase their visibility at civic and non-governmental organisations, the women go in traditional dress with their children on their backs, address the meeting in Xhosa, and ululate if they are unhappy about the procedure used or decisions made.

In preparation for negotiations with local, provincial, and national governments they role-play the situation and each member of the team is well informed about the issues and the questions to ask. The proposed responses to officials are rehearsed before hand.

They have learned these tactics from their culture, schooling, and experience in agricultural projects in the rural areas, and from their experiences as political activists. They have also had opportunities to swap stories with national and international housing savings groups.

BUILDING HOUSES

The women learned the initial lessons of surveying, planning, and other tasks in building houses from networks in India with which the VMHDA has had exchanges. This helped to demystify the tasks ahead and showed them that unschooled women can learn to build their own homes.

Some of the women like Mama Msiza learned brick making from companies. Tata Sigebe, who learned his trade in Gauteng, has passed on his building skills to many women. But the injustices of the apartheid past and of job reservation are severely felt, as the VM project could not find skilled builders from the immediate community to draw in.

The first exercise in the process of building a house is designing their dream houses from cardboard boxes. The second is learning to measure and cost the house. This lengthy process must be accurate. The trainer begins with the person's knowledge and slowly more complex measurements are taught. The trainer uses visual and physical measurements within the new home builder's understanding and costs it according to these familiar measurements (People's Dialogue, September 1994:6). For example, the trainer will say:

> It's like baking a cake where we use cups and spoons. But with this bigger cake we use hands, feet, bags of cement, wheelbarrows and bricks.

Teams construct the house, with the more experienced members leading the group.

MONITORING AND EVALUATION

In monitoring and evaluating this project, I collected data through in-depth individual and group interviews and took note of the following:

- There are no unproblematic qualitative indicators for measuring gender awareness, empowerment and the impact of such awareness in the household.
- The development of these qualities is a process that is not linear and is dependent on the individual.
- The women have no stated objectives to transform class and gender relations and take up these issues as they arise through collective and participatory action.

- Theirs is essentially a grassroots, bottom-up, self-help approach to action and development, which has achieved wide linkages, international support, and national political influence. Their philosophy of development is heavily grounded in the experience of poor exploited women. The themes include exploitative customary laws, husbands, and employers (Duke,1995:62). They carry the burdens of the family.

- They emphasise their need to appear politically neutral so that they can interact with government structures on local and provincial levels and be able to organise in most poor communities regardless of political affiliation.

- They monitor and evaluate themselves in terms of their slogan "We build houses, people and communities."

The achievements of the project and developmental areas that can be assessed using quantitative or qualitative measures are:

- Amount of land obtained
- The number of houses built
- Security and stability of community
- Impact on state policy on financing and provision of low cost housing

In terms of impact on gender relations and empowerment of women:

- Women's control over resources
- Women's freedom of speech,
- Women's control over their bodies
- Women's freedom of movement
- Improvement in self-confidence and pride
- Development and emergence of leadership skills
- Gender relations and attitudinal changes of men

Development Objectives

Acquiring Land and Building Houses

The Federation discussed the critical issues of land tenure and women's rights to land with the Department of Land Affairs. The VMHDA felt that land for housing had taken a second priority. Local councilors often claimed that the ownership of land is unknown and so they cannot release it for housing development. On the other hand, the VMHDA's campaign for land from the Catholic Church was successful. They demonstrated to the Church and other non-governmental organisations (NGOs) that they are capable of developing the land. Recently, they got a loan from the Land Bank and purchased additional land for the next phase of the housing project.

In the first phase, 140 houses were constructed in Philippi and another 61 houses in Macassar. A community centre, day-care centre, and infrastructure for water, sanitation, electricity and roads were also constructed by the women.

The women have been able to build their homes for far less than private developers charge and within the limits of the subsidy (R17 500). Rose Maso exclaims:

> I never knew in my life that I could have a house made of bricks that I have built myself and [which] costs less [than I thought]. It is a miracle to have this house today. I keep asking myself, "Is this really my house?"

Security and Stability of the Community

The democratic structures and decision-making give the members a sense of security. No one feels left out. Problems that can give rise to conflict are identified and resolved collectively. The VMHDA is functionally organised into several working committees, which reflect the amount of work needed to organise a housing project from conception to completion, including collecting savings, managing pooled resources, negotiating for finance and land, dealing with government red-tape, planning and building houses. The committees are:

- The Trust Committee supervises the development process and negotiates for grants and loans.
- The Land Committee negotiates land titles.

- The Treasury Committee manages the savings of the group.
- The House Model Committee facilitates housing design.
- The Survey Committee gathers the socioeconomic data of the groups.
- The Catering Committee arranges functions for visiting groups.
- The Building Co-op Committee costs building material and builds houses.
- The Networking Committee liaises with other savings groups and co-ordinates the exchanges of skills training. Often, when other groups are experiencing problems, the network will send a representative to help sort out problems.
- The Gardening Committee, a recent addition, organises the planting of trees, fruits, and vegetables.

Most decisions are made by the whole group at the weekly general meeting attended by about 150 women. According to Patricia, any item can be brought to this meeting. Women have organised their households to expect them not to return home after work, so husbands take charge of cooking and child-care on this night. Family members of households are welcome to attend the meeting. There is a sense that empowerment occurs through discussion and the involvement of members in all the activities of the organisation. However, active attendance and participation in the group's activities is one of the criteria taken into account when the VMHDA considers an application for a loan.

The women are proud of the organisation's participatory and democratic way of operating. The process of collective decision making, problem solving, and working in teams has given the women a lot of confidence and strength to challenge existing power-blocks and to actively participate in civic and social projects and activities.

Rose Maso, a member of the management committee, says " We are sometimes faced with problems but we normally sit down as a committee and discuss those problems. Each person would give her view and we try to resolve the problem because we have formed this organisation for a certain purpose. The reason we are here is housing only."

Transparency is a key feature of the organisation. A meticulous accounting system is kept in which are recorded individual payments and withdrawals. These are circulated to all the savings groups on a regular basis. In this way, each individual has full knowledge of the financial status of the organisation.

Impact on State Policy on Financing and Provision of Houses

The VMHDA has pursued a careful and sustained strategy of critical engagement with government, showing the government how the savings scheme works and how the government can support them. They have invited government officials to visit various branches and view their achievements. In November 1997, the Victoria Mxenge community celebrated the completion of the first phase of building by inviting sister organisations and national, provincial, and local government officials to a feast. Housing Minister Sanki Mthembi-Nkondo expressed her support for the project and was promptly asked to concretise this with a further donation of R10 million.

During the speeches, the women of Victoria Mxenge made certain that the ministers heard their demands for more land, additional schools, and health clinics in the new community. The other purpose of such meetings is to demonstrate that poor people are far more capable than officials recognise. But government and financial institutions need to understand and support these developmental processes through finance and enabling legislation.

The project has influenced state policy to a certain extent. The bureaucratic process of obtaining financial subsidies has been simplified and speeded up. The women of VMHDA have successfully petitioned for old age pensioners to get subsidies. They have succeeded in negotiating to submit standardised building plans and to pay a reduced fee to the local council for the approval of the building plans.

Today, the VMHDA enjoys significant moral support from all levels of government and from both the Departments of Housing and Land Affairs. However, there is a feeling among many members of the Federation that the government does not consider their involvement as that of an equal partner, but wants to control resources and the pace of development. Thus, Ted Baumann of the People's Dialogue (Cape Argus, May 24, 1997) insists that "Victoria Mxenge has gotten off the ground despite the government, not because of government assistance."

Gender Issues

Control over resources

Through the project, the women have become the official registered owners of their houses. The women have also gained control over financial resources as they apply for subsidies and loans and are responsible for paying off the loans through the savings schemes.

In 1998, the organisation made the decision to inform all husbands that the houses were to be registered in their wives' names as the latter are responsible for paying back the loan, applying for the subsidy, and paying for basic services and rates. This decision represents a major shift in the organisation's discourse, as previously women were loath to do this last their husbands subject them to violent abuse, leave them, or reduce financial contributions to the household. Conflicts arising from the decision were managed by the older women who spoke to difficult husbands. Some marriages were strengthened while others broke down.

FREEDOM OF SPEECH AND MOVEMENT

The acknowledgement of women's ownership and control over vital resources has shifted the gender balance as women can now participate in most of the activities of the project. In addition, it has given the women freedom of speech and movement and control over their reproductive decisions. For example, they can leave messages with their children for irate husbands when they are away at meetings; they have gained their husband or partner's support for the project; and they can discuss family planning and sometimes choose the method of contraception.

SELF-CONFIDENCE

The process of learning to dream, save, keep records, and then build has given women a sense of self-confidence and empowerment that has exceeded their own expectations. The skills they have learned, such as financial office management, building and buying skills, have encouraged them to continue, in spite of the often frustrating slowness of the housing and infrastructure development process. The emphasis on everyone's being a part of the process and on their leadership skills has set the framework for a cohesive set of relationships and given most women a sense of pride and empowerment. As Veliswa says, "Today I can build a house from the bottom up. I never thought I could do that in my life, so I hope that in this new South Africa we will be able to learn and build it up."

LEADERSHIP

The leadership of the organisation is exceptional. Patricia, one of the founding members, is highly committed and dedicated to the housing savings scheme and to the improvement of the living conditions of poor people. So are the leaders of the Homeless Peoples Federation, Peoples Dialogue, and the NGOs with whom they have had exchanges, notably Mahila Milan of India.

The strategy of continuous training has helped to prevent the consolidation of resources in the hands of a few dominant leaders. Knowledge of the basic principles is widespread and local leaders have been developed. They in turn train more people locally, nationally and internationally.

In October 1997, the VMHDA won an award from the United Nations (UN) Development Programme for taking significant strides to eradicate poverty. In 1996, at the UN Habitat Conference in Istanbul, the VMHDA received a standing ovation for their presentation on women-delivered housing.

Gender relations and attitudinal changes of men

The women have broken through traditional barriers, such as customary laws relating to land rights and ownership of land and property. Through their activities, they have challenged the traditional power relationships within their marriages and dispelled the idea that women are inferior. They are strongly driven by the need to give their children decent places to grow up in and to transform the hostile urban environment in which they find themselves.

The following quotes from the women themselves demonstrate some aspects of changed gender relationships:

> NOKHANGELANI: Men must know we are their left-hand partners because they stay in the house built by us. Our husbands see that the houses are ready. Before they thought we were lying, but now they have visions of themselves in the new houses.
>
> XOLISWA: It is not so easy for them to kick you out because you have built the house, so you are strong in the marriage.
>
> MAMA MSIZA: This project builds married life because the whole family gets involved in building the house. The marriage grows stronger because people are working with and not against each other.

In the beginning, Patricia was the target of angry husbands who objected to her political involvement and the fact that she was an unmarried mother. She organised house meetings with the men and encouraged them to take an active interest in the savings scheme by pointing to the fact that in rural areas it is the women who build the homes. This approach won her their confidence and respect (Ismail, 1996:4).

Women have been empowered not only in the home, but also in male-dominated organisations such as those of building and design experts, political organisations, and community organisations.

In brief, this project illustrates the interconnections between women's education and empowerment, the attributes of collective strength, and individual self-reliance (Medel-Añonuevo, 1997).

CRITICISMS

The criticisms leveled at the organisation come from communities who feel that the government should be the main agent responsible for the delivery of houses and basic services. These communities have no access to land, cannot afford to buy land at market prices, and without land tenure, cannot apply for subsidies. They feel the initiative of VMHDA takes pressure and responsibility for housing provision away from the government.

Moreover, the sustainability of the project is being questioned as the process is slow and the capacity to save is adversely affected by spiraling costs.

These criticisms are directly linked to the government's failure to integrate the VMHDA system into the mainstream of its delivery process. It has failed to interact constructively with the VMHDA on a number of issues such as providing basic services and making land available.

Through the Reconstruction and Development Programme (RDP) and Masakhane, the government has constructed a language of people's empowerment and support for the poor. The RDP has committed itself to building a million houses by the year 2000. However, according to an urban planner from the city council, "Unfortunately it has not built many houses in Cape Town and is at the tail end of the process of housing delivery."

The government has provided a political context in which the vision of the women of VMHDA can be realised. This positive context is useful in giving the women moral support but they also need government to deliver in concrete ways. A government that seeks partnerships with self-help development projects for political purposes must also do its part to maintain those partnerships. The women say of the government's attitude: "We lit the match, now where is the firewood?" (People's Dialogue, June 1996: 29).

The women of Victoria Mxenge are attempting to meet a basic need and right to shelter amidst many difficulties. They are strong, visionary and determined, and they are admired by many people from different quarters because their commitment to social action has borne fruit.

NOTES

1. Recently the women of the VMHDA trained many men from other savings groups. A lot of time has to be spent teaching men to work like they do, slowly, in order that others can learn from observing them. The men have to learn not to waste materials and to be accurate in their measurements. Patricia explains that this is because men have often worked for big companies where speed is important and where there is much wastage.

2. People's Dialogue on Land and Shelter is a non-governmental organisation which explores ways for giving support to homeless urban dwellers internationally so that they may address their own housing needs.

3. The South African Homeless Federation (SAHPF) was established in 1994 and has a membership of 30,000. It grew out of a network of savings schemes with a focus on making credit available for development and involved mainly women.

4. The international organisations that VMHDA networks with are: Mahila Milan from India, Women's Bank in Sri Lanka, Lumanti in Nepal, Squatters and Urban Poor Federation in Cambodia, the Asian Coalition for Housing Rights in Thailand, and Cearah Periferia in Brazil. These community organisations are involved in savings and credit schemes to mobilise communities. The organisations are not exactly similar, however. For example, some savings schemes are coupled with micro-enterprises.

5. The Housing Budget was cut by R1.8 billion this year. The explanation given was that the Ministry had underspent the housing budget last year. This year's budget is 1.8 percent compared to 3.4 percent for 1995/1996.

WORKS CITED

Cross, M. and Friedman, M. 1997. *Women, Land and Authority*. In Meer, S. (ed). London: Oxford University Press.

Dankelman, J. and Davidson, J. 1987. *Women and Environment in the Third World*. Earthscan Publication.

Duke, C. 1995. "Review of the Indian SEWA Movement." In *Convergence*, 31, 3.

Ismail, S. 1996. "Patricia Zukiswa Matolengwe: An Inspiration to All." In *Development Poverty Profile*, 4. IDASA.

Medel-Añonuevo, C. 1997. "Learning Gender Justice: The Challenge for Adult Education in the 21st Century." In *Adult Education and Development*, No. 49. pp. 81-90.

Peoples' Dialogue. (June 1994). "A model home, the story of homeless women." Cape Town.

People's Dialogue. (September 1994). "Regaining knowledge, an appeal to abandon illusions, innovative community-based shelter training programmes." Cape Town.

People's Dialogue. (June 1996). "Bojang Bo A Bua." Cape Town.

The Housing Act cited in the *Government Gazette* (19 December 1997), No.18521. Pretoria, South Africa.

The Equality Clause cited in the *Redefined Working Draft New Constitution*, 4th edition (18 March 1996). Constituent Assembly, Cape Town.

White, C. 1993: "'Close to home" in Johannesburg: Gender Oppression in Township Households." In *Women's Studies International Forum*, 16, 2.

INTERVIEWS

This article is based on in-depth individual and group interviews held over a few years with members of the VMHDA. All the interviews were recorded and transcribed. The interviews took place at Victoria Mxenge. The group interviews were conducted in Xhosa with an interpreter from outside the organisation.

> Patricia Matolengwe was interviewed on 27 August 1996, 18 July 1997 and 14 April 1998, and 12 February 1999.

> Nokhangelani Roji, Veliswa Mbeki and Xoliswa Tiso were interviewed on 4 November 1996.

> Mama Msiza, Rose Maso, Sylvia Qoma, and Tata Sigebe were interviewed on 11 November 1996.

> Rose Maso, Nokhangelani Roji and Veliswa Mbeki were interviewed on 16 July 1998 and 12 February 1999.

> The author attended two of the organisation's general meetings—on 23 October 1996 and on 16 July 1997—to request permission to write this article as well as to verify information received from interviews.

THE MAHILA SAMAKHYA EXPERIENCE

Lakshmi Krishnamurty

INTRODUCTION

The Mahila Samakhya (MS) Programme, also known as "Education for Women's Equality," was started in 1989 by the Department of Education of the Ministry of Human Resource Development of the Government of India. It began in four states and now covers some 4,000 to 5,000 villages in eight states.

It is administered by a society, a general council (National Resource Group), and executive committees whose members are drawn from government and from a variety of non-government organizations (including universities, NGOs, and journalists). This provides a wide platform for debate and makes possible a certain flexibility of administration, which is a factor essential to the implementation of a programme like Mahila Samakhya.

The main objective of Mahila Samakhya is to initiate a process where women will perceive the need to move from a state of passive acceptance of their life situation to one of active self-determination and control over their lives and their immediate environment. Basic to the process is the enhancement of the self-confidence and self-image of the participants, who are rural poor women. The main instrument for achieving the objectives of the programme is the Mahila Sangha, a women's collective at the village level.

The programme conceives of education as the development of life skills, and not just literacy. This kind of education would not only enable women to become aware of their rights but also, through the collective strength of the Sangha, make effective action possible for the realization of their rights, beginning with having a voice in the family and community. Literacy is only one of the programme's resources that the women might decide to access. There are no child care centres or savings fund, nor other related services. This is so that attention is not diverted from the central focus of enabling women to develop the feeling of "I am" and "I can do".

Education in the MS context means:

- Acquiring self-confidence and esteem.
- Becoming able to deal with authority in the home, in the community, in government offices.
- Knowing about one's own body, about health problems and remedies; and being able to apply this knowledge in daily life.
- Learning vocational skills.
- Knowing about the law and being able to use the legal system to redress wrongs.
- Reading and writing, since literacy is part of education.

For the programme, losing one's feelings of helplessness and becoming empowered to say "I can change" or "I can bring about change" is the ideal "result" of education. An awareness of the self as a human being with the same rights as other human beings is what Mahila Samakhya education hopes to instill in its women clients.

There are three different but related aspects of education: 1) education as life skills; 2) education as information/knowledge; and 3) education as literacy.

EDUCATION AS LIFE SKILLS

It is indisputable that the basis of managing life (as opposed to life managing one) is confidence and self-esteem. The participants in the MS programme know this, as the following representative voices show.

I EXIST

"By being a member of the Sangha we have gotten a 'name' where no name existed before."

LOSS OF FEAR

"We didn't know what a Sangha was and we were scared to talk to village elders. When anyone visited our village, we never spoke to them. The village elders dealt with them. Now with the Sangha, we have gained strength and courage. Now the village elders approach us regarding various issues like rations, roads, etc."

"Now we are able to face and talk with the police and other people in authority without hesitation."

Expanding Horizons

"Earlier we only knew our parental home and in-law home. Now we go to many places."

Collective Strength

"The strength we have comes from being all together; it comes from the feeling that we belong to a Sangha."

"When we want to achieve something, we all sit and think about it, plan for it, and then take the necessary action. The villagers are a little in awe of us."

"Everywhere we go, we acknowledge the fact that we are Sangha members."

Respect

"We convinced our menfolk at home to let us join the Sangha. Now we get.respect at home."

"Before they used to treat us like dirt. Now we have a standing of our own ."

Making Things Happen

"The village people come to us with their problems, e.g., if the ANIVI (Auxilliary Nurse/Midwife) does not come regularly; when village development activities are not carried out properly; or when there is trouble at home."

"We listen and we talk and we do things. People believe in us."

Decision-Making and Planning for the Future

"Now we take part in deciding things for our children. We do not want our daughters to be like us. They will study and do lots of things. We have begun only now but they will begin early."

Rights and Action for Change

"Recognizing that I have rights and can take action towards getting these rights has widened to include the village. MS women, supported by their Sanghas, have been elected to Panchayats, in pursuit of change at the community and village level."

Education as Information

Education for life skills underlies all MS activities and is largely communicated through non-verbal means and interactive behaviour. However, a large part of MS education focuses on the acquisition and effective application of information and knowledge. This aspect of education has been separated from literacy because many Sangha women, in spite of being illiterate or only marginally literate, assimilate vast quantities of information at workshops and meetings. This information is regularly applied in everyday life, specifically, in the areas of health, environment, law, and government programmes.

The demystification of knowledge distilled as information not only enables women to take action themselves (e.g., with reference to traditional medicine and health practices) but also makes accessible the primary health care center, the *anganwadi*, the school, the Block Development Officer's office, the bank, the police station, the courts, etc. Literacy is not experienced as essential to "making things happen" in all these arenas that matter, as the story below shows.

> Rukma, 45 years old, of Saharanpur District, had been working with Mahila Samakhya for some time. She had attended many meetings and training workshops. On May 16,1993, Rukma went to a nearby village to buy rations from the weekly *haat* (market). By the time she had completed her work, she found that the last bus for her village had left. It was getting dark and she decided to walk home. After a while she noticed Raja, 22 years old following her. Soon he caught up with her and managed to overcome and rape her. Rukma's only witnesses were the potatoes and carrots strewn on the road.
>
> Nevertheless, Rukma managed to return home to her husband. Together they went to the village Pradhan (headman) and gave details of the assault. At break of day, with her soiled clothes in a bag for evidence and without a bath, Rukma went to lodge a complaint at the police station with a Sahayogini. The policeman didn't realize that he was dealing with women who were aware of "what has to be done" in case of a rape. As he wrote up the case, he was surprised that Rukma knew what to write in the complaint. The women noticed that the policeman didn't seal Rukma's clothes. (for use as evidence).. The Sahayoginii and Rukma realized that there was a great gap between the law on paper and its actual practice.

Finally, they went to the doctor to ask him to conduct a medical examination for proof of rape. The doctor was not keen but after much cajoling, he conducted the examination. However, he did not give Rukma a copy of the medical report. Meanwhile, hearing about Rukma's action, Raja fled the village. The police cajoled his mother to come to the police station. The women, on the other hand, did not want the old lady to be harassed for her son's doing. Finally, when Raja did not turn up, the Sakhis waited with his mother at the police station. Eventually Raja surrendered to the police. The villagers then put great pressure on Rukma to withdraw the case. According to them, Raja had already paid the penalty for his crime. He had been arrested for a day and his name was listed in the police records. Both Rukma and Raja were poor and could not afford a long court case. Eventually the Sangha women decided it was best to accept Raja's public apology. The next day, in front of the lawyers within the court premises, the Sangha women made Raja apologize (in writing on stamped paper) and promise that he would never rape another woman again.

Rukma and the Sahayogini knew every step that had to be taken in case of rape. Neither the policeman nor the doctor could fool them.

Here is another story to illustrate the point.

When a visiting Education Officer (EO) told Sakhi Santa Ben of Leelavanti Mahila Sangha of Gujarat MS that there is no official rule authorizing deductions from students' scholarships, she passed on this information to her village Sangha. The Sangha women later confronted a teacher in the presence of the EO. The students revealed that the teacher was taking Rs.10 from each student. The EO immediately issued orders for the teacher's dismissal. The teacher asked for another chance. The Sangha women then asked the EO to give the teacher the opportunity to correct his conduct, to which the EO agreed. The teacher promised the Sangha women in writing that there would not be any misdeed on his part in the future.

This case (and many others like it) exemplifies strategies used by the Sangha to set things right. The correct procedure was followed: information was obtained and the "proper channel", the EO, was contacted. No feathers were ruffled. It is worth noting that the teacher was not terminated.

Many times, Sangha women have taken action fully armed with information and supported by other women. They have not always been successful. Nor have they always balanced blind justice with understanding. But there has been enough success to make women confident of their action methodologies.

Education as Literacy

The Sangha women consider literacy to be desirable, but more for their children than for themselves. This is perhaps due to the fact that some of the more telling outcomes of education—i.e., feeling empowered, gaining knowledge, being able to get things done—are things women have experienced without becoming literate.

However, sometimes literacy becomes necessary, as the following case illustrates:

> An elected Panchayat member, Balamma of Hireven Kelkunta, Raichur District, Karnataka was campaigning to become president. One day, three men came to her and informed her that a meeting was being held in the next taluk and she had to attend it. They made her sign some papers. She readily signed without reading the contents. They then took her to Raichur by jeep. There they left her in a hut and said that the jeep had broken down. Suspecting something fishy, she demanded to be taken home. When she reached home the next evening she was informed that the other male candidate had been elected president unopposed. She consulted the District Commissioner about her problem. He expressed his helplessness as she had "signed" the withdrawal papers without reading them.

This was certainly incentive enough for Balamma to become literate!

INPUTS

The two concrete inputs into the Mahila Samakhya Programme are the Mahila Kutir, or the women's hut/cottage, and the Mahila Sikshan Kendra, the Women's Study Centre. The Mahila Kutir is a "space" for women to come together. The Mahila Sikshan Kendra, on the other hand, runs residential educational courses for women for periods varying between three and 12 months depending on the state office's decision. This in turn is based on the participating women's convenience.

Besides providing basic literacy and course work equivalent to the formal school's 5th to 8th class, the education programme concentrates on reproductive health, legal rights, karate and anything that will lift the spirits and enhance the self-image of the girls and women attending the Mahila Sikshan Kendra.

The course has been so successful that participants, who are pale, frightened, and homesick in the beginning, howl when it is time to go home, for this has been that once in a lifetime experience of no responsibility and freedom to laugh and shout, run and. gossip. To capture what has changed and the impact—that is the challenge for the Mahila Samakhya.

The Sangha (Collective) is central to the functioning of Mahila Samakhya. The Sanghas were initiated and later nurtured by the Sahayoginis (literally, one who gives support), who are middle-level workers, each in charge of 10 villages. The Sahayoginis receive intensive training, initially in self-development, interpersonal relationships, and feminist theory as related to existing realities in their own environment. Subsequently, they receive training in legal matters, alternative medicine, and other topics that the different State programmes consider necessary. The Sahayoginis are the main conduit of information for the Sangha women.

At first, when Sahayoginis went into villages to initiate Sangha formation, they met with a lot of suspicion. They were not offering any incentives; they were not talking of education or even the ubiquitous family planning. They merely wanted women to come together to talk. There are innumerable proverbs and sayings to the effect that women talk too much! So why this special effort to bring then together just to talk, the community asked. The Sahayoginis despaired, but persisted.

Much of the early period was fun and enjoyment. A year after the programme started, when women were asked what the programme was all about, they said it was singing and dancing, drawing, painting and laughing. And of course, talking. Through all these, women were discovering themselves and gaining self-confidence. They were also sharing their joys and sorrows and finding solace and strength in the sharing. However, awareness of capabilities and possibilities is not enough. It must lead to action.

Sangha women have taken action—in different directions. They have not only experienced their new found strength, but also added to it through experience. In particular, they have learned to fight for their rights.

ACCESS TO RESOURCES

BASIC AMENITIES

The Sangha women have used their collective strength to demand basic amenities like water, health and economic benefits made available by government. In village Pal of Rajkot District, Gujarat, water taps had been provided for the convenience of the whole village. However, the arrangement of water distribution was such that Patells (an upper caste) were getting more water, and supply was negligible or sometimes nil in Harijan (lower caste) localities. Sangha women were upset about this system of water distribution. They kept thinking about how they could alter the existing situation.

Sangha members called a meeting and discussed the water problem. It was decided that they first meet the Sarpanch (head of the Panchayat). They had a talk with the Sarpanch who was not very co-operative. He was from a higher caste.

The women thought that they would have to go to the district level. They all went by tractor to the district headquarters and met the Collector, who then put pressure on the officers of the *taluka* to call a Gram Sabha (village meeting) and discuss the problem.

The Sangha women argued that since they also pay water tax, they should also get water. It was decided that when water distribution takes place, two women from the Sangha would also be there to see to it that the water is equally distributed. After some time, the arrangement was regularized.

Water is one, if not the main issue addressed by Sangha women in all MS areas. Many of the cases are about unequal availability of water on a caste and class basis. By and large, the women work on the authorities to see that justice is done, rather than take the law into their own hands. Negotiation is part of the MS strategy to make the administration responsible and accountable to the people.

Other basic amenities that Sangha women have organized themselves for, usually successfully, are streetlights, roads, drains, electricity, ration shops, increase in the number and frequency of bus routes, hand pumps, latrines, and safe school buildings. This has happened in almost all villages where there are strong Sanghas. Conversely, these activities are missing where the Sanghas are weak or have fallen apart for some reason.

TRADITIONAL MEDICINE

An empowering experience has been the collection of information about and use of traditional medicine. Traditional medical practices are doubly important in the absence of allopathic medical facilities. The affirmation of known practices helps empower the women even more.

Economic Resources

The women of the Sangha also assert their right to access economic resources, which can be categorized thus: 1) fair/higher wages; 2) government schemes; and 3) savings and thrift.

Next to water, wages is perhaps the most common issue around which women have organized themselves.

In one village in Gujarat, Sangha women successfully campaigned for better wages. The prices for essentials had gone up and the women at a Sangha meeting felt that during the peak season of the harvest at least, their wages should be higher. The women decided that they should get a minimum of Rs.30 per day as wages; they should be provided with afternoon meals and tea should be given twice a day.

To protest their existing low wages, all the women decided not to go to work. The landlord called a meeting with the women, who then told him about their decision. Outraged, the landlord sent for women labourers from the neighboring village. However, the Sangha women had already informed the Sangha women of Dhokra regarding their move.

The women of both villages were united and none went came to work in the fields. They decided to fight the unjust level of wages. "We would rather die of starvation than work on such low wages," they said. On the third day, the landlords begged them to come. The women set down their conditions to which the landlords had to agree and the Sangha won.

In some cases, the women have held out for two to three months at a time. In some cases they do not succeed, but often they do. While the struggle is on, other women in the village help out with food. Hearing of successful cases from other areas help to keep spirits from flagging.

In other places, there have been struggles for equal wages with men. Where successful, men often subsequently demand a rise in their wages too!

In the case of government schemes (including credit from National Banks), only some women are selected for credit on a quota basis while the majority of Sangha women do not benefit. At times, this has threatened to break up the Sangha. On the other hand, women have refused schemes/loans because not all of them could benefit. This is a very delicate balancing act between the individual and the group. There are no ready answers, especially in the situation of deprivation in which most Sangha women live.

Savings and thrift are not the most important activities of these self-help groups. This is perhaps because the central tenet of MS philosophy and practice is the collective strength of Sangha members in fighting against the inequality and oppression contained in many areas of daily life. The general experience in MS regarding savings and thrift is that it is detrimental to Sangha coherence, especially if the activity is introduced in the early days of Sangha formation. Accessing resources is a relatively easy task compared to dealing with the core of gender inequality—the violence that is perpetrated on women. By accessing resources, especially tangible material resources, women actually enlist the community on their side since water, roads and loans, are shared assets. However, the problem of gender inequality is often not addressed or is marginalised.

WOMEN AND VIOLENCE

Violence against women emerges as a truly universal issue in Mahila Samakhya. From the outset, it was recognized as a non-negotiable point around which Sangha women thought it necessary to reflect and act. The records show that women's groups in every *taluka* in MS Districts have at some point or other demonstrated strongly against violence against women, and on many occasions managed to have the culprits have been punished. But it is equally true that no barrier to committing violence against women has been created. Cases of rape, murder and battering occur despite all resistance.

Violence against women appears to be the hardest ground to break. However, there is a steady, positive shift at two levels, which can be taken as indicators of the maturity of understanding and responses of Sangha women to issues of violence. First, they have moved towards a deeper understanding of what hurts and humiliates women. Second, they have learned to react against caste discrimination as violence at the basic human level—i.e., humiliation and injury to the personhood of all subordinated groups.

A significant change wrought by Mahila Samakhya in its members is the consensus about what constitutes violence despite differences in idiom and in the degrees of significance accorded to the "line items" listed under the category of violence. The aggregated list that has emerged from meetings held with Sangha women and Sahayoginis is as follows:

- wife beating
- rape
- mental torture: forcing women to obey and accept in an unquestioning manner
- humiliating treatment of infertile women and calling them "barren"
- the *devadasi* (traditional prostitutes dedicated to god) tradition

- inhuman treatment of widows: isolation and segregation
- labelling defiant, non-conforming women as *"udayan"* (witches)
- eve-teasing
- forced abortions and female infanticide
- humiliation of wives when they don't please their husbands

The Sahyoginis now note a major shift in how Sangha women perceive violence. During the initial Mahila Samakhya training sessions, the women almost always shared agonizing personal experiences by describing them as *"dukh"* or suffering that "women have to go through" because they are women. For them, physical and emotional vulnerability were intimately connected aspects of what they considered to be "the tragedy of womanhood". This suffering, pain, and sense of vulnerability was seen as cutting across caste, class, and rural and urban divides. Now, with their deepened understanding of the basic dignity of a person, these and similar experiences have been renamed as "violence" against women.

The change in term signals the realization that women have rights as persons and that they do not have to put up with discrimination of whatever form. Thus, in a community where MS had been working primarily with Basawa jati women, a man who was very rude to the Sahayogini and who used foul, abusive language was brought before the village elders by Sangha women. They also filed a case against the man with the local police. In the course of discussions, it was found that the man concerned had bribed the police (by paying them Rs.300) The village community then decided that there was no point in waiting for the police to take action. They further decided that the culprit should pay a fine of Rs.600, which is double the amount he paid as bribe, and each woman from the Sangha would be allowed to beat the man twice with her sandals. The women welcomed the decision taken by the village elders, and agreed that the penalty of Rs.600 should be imposed. However, they decided not to beat up the man.

Noteworthy is the fact that the Sangha women could now call a meeting of the entire village community on an issue which they think is important and get a decision in their favour. But even more significant is the fact that the Sangha acted on an issue which a few years back was not considered a major affront. *Gali*, or abusive language, was generally seen as a very trivial matter. But the Sangha woman reflected on the matter and declared that the use of foul language violates the dignity of a woman and is therefore totally unacceptable behaviour. The fact that they chose not to beat up the culprit with sandals, in spite of getting the sanction from the community at large, demonstrates their own style of settling issues and their confidence in demonstrating their sense of justice.

The shift from recognizing only gross forms of violence to a subtler sensitivity to the dignity women underscores the renewed self-image of rural women. In some areas, Nad Adalats or Women's Courts have been set up. It is emerging as an alternative forum for justice where women can talk fearlessly about themselves and seek justice as a "right".

The fact that such fora function publicly with an ever-growing number of cases, points to how families are making public that which used to be kept strictly a family secret. This in turn means that the woman is no longer considered solely to blame for rape, harassment, etc. The community, through the Gram Panchayat or council of elders, is acknowledging that the harassment of women is wrong, and the perpetrators of this violence should be punished. This is a stronger indicator of change than settling a case in court, because the law is often ahead of existing social mores and does not reflect real social change as much as actual community action does.

An inter-state comparison shows that cases of violence that come into the open are almost always those involving a man from outside the immediate family. Intra-family violence is dealt with more discreetly while rape and harassment in public places are dealt with publicly. Moreover, the women report a decline in domestic violence (although there is no statistical data to support this), perhaps because of the improved status of the women in the community (i.e., they are consulted on community issues; they attend meetings and workshops; they have introduced improvements to community life). "He [her husband] now thinks I am a human being, too," one woman said. It would seem that directly confronting the issue of violence in the home is extremely threatening. It can lead to family break-ups, which stirs up deep insecurities for both men and women.

THE MANY DIMENSIONS OF POWER

So far we have looked at how empowerment has been operative in the daily lives of the Sangha women. What is the texture of this empowerment and how does it operate in the different arenas of women's lives? How do women handle power? Do women in a man's world follow given patterns of power play? Does a critical mass (as opposed to individual and small groups) of women behave differently? What has "empowerment" meant to Sangha women? What has happened to the age-old internalized self-image of the self-sacrificing, nurturing, and ignorant woman in the face of the women's newly acquired ability to "make things happen"?

These are not new questions to which there is one clean, easy answer. The MS experience shows that the Sangha women have acted in different ways, including continuing to stay oppressed and taking on the attitudes of power they see around them.

However, most of the Sangha women who have felt empowered have acted in practical ways—giving a little, taking a little; making two steps forward and taking one step back. They have negotiated rather than confronted; maintained relationships rather than acted in terms of ultimate and abstract "truths". This is visible in their encounter with the community and now, increasingly, with *panchayats*. The home, their immediate political arena, appears to be the "last frontier" of change.

The following story from Karnataka captures the essence of the MS experience of women's use of power.

> In the village of Yediapur, Raichur District, a research study was to be carried out about women's status in Karnataka. The survey was being done in collaboration with Sangha members. For some reason, some villagers disrupted the survey, were rude to the investigators, and put a halt to the interviews being conducted. The survey team left. As the hosts of the visiting team, the Sangha members felt that they had been humiliated by their co-villagers.
>
> Among the leaders of the group who had insulted the research team were three village hotel owners who refused to admit scheduled castes and tribes within the premises of their hotels. Angered by the behaviour of the villagers, particularly of the hotel owners, the Sangha women confronted them. "So far we have not said anything to you," the women said. "But now we will see that you admit everybody to your hotels."
>
> The women asked the Tehsildar to close down the hotels. "It is against the law to practice such discrimination," they said.
>
> Subsequently, one of the hoteliers came to them and pleaded that he had no other way of earning a living and feeding his family. He agreed to serve everyone who came to the hotel. The women talked this matter over among themselves and decided that he should be allowed "to carry on business but must serve everybody."

This case demonstrates the newfound confidence of Sangha women to take action to right what they consider to be a wrong, even if it means confronting the entire village. The Sangha women did not take the law into their own hands. They merely saw to it that the law was implemented, an undertaking that can be more difficult than taking the law into one's hands.

Having done this, they nonetheless demonstrated compassion for the hotelier who had no other means of living. They promoted justice tempered with common sense and understanding. By agreeing that the hotelier open shop, they also bargained for admitting everyone. It is through such balancing acts that the Sangha women keep themselves within the periphery of village goodwill, while advancing their cause in small but sure steps. One can discern in this case a pattern of alternative use of power, which is not overpowering or "destructive" of others.

The MS experience from all states broadly demonstrates three stages in the process of shedding off powerlessness. These are not chronological stages, and are in fact intertwined in the continuous struggle for change in women's position at home, in the community, and in society as a whole.

The first stage of empowerment involves the ability to distance themselves from a given situation and recognize the structures of power, decode its symbols, and look into them without fear. This may not alter the situation at all, but it alters the chemistry of the encounter. Women learn to analyze the situation and in the process, their "fear" gradually turns into an "understanding". This can only happen when they discover that their personal suffering is a "kind" of systematic phenomenon, a chronic situation, which need not cripple their morale.

The next stage in this process is resistance. They realize that what is not "right" need not be accepted. Together, as members of a collective, they develop the courage to protest.

At the third stage a more mature state of realization emerges: viz. that we need to know more, learn more, find out more before making simplistic judgements. Basic confidence in oneself generated by continuous support from a group nurtures the learning spirit and humility in one's own position.

In contrast, there are numerous cases of the same Sangha women quietly enduring family violence. What they do with ease in a public forum is a most difficult personal battle at home. "We confront men outside but it is a no-win situation with our own family members at times," they admit. Women who are towers of strength in public appear willing to put up with beating and being cowed at home.

It is easier to effect changes outside the home where the collective can visibly be together. In most community level action, the women are able to deviate from traditional ways because they are acting together in a critical mass; unlike at home where they battle the very roots of power, ultimately, alone. Also, whether it is wage, caste, or other struggles, women have tempered justice with their conditioned reflexes of nurturance. And so it is that in the family, while they put up with abuse, they are also beginning to insist that their daughters go to school.

However, these and other changes in the power structure of the family are difficult to observe and record, much less achieve. Apart from the Sanghas, there are many fora in the MS districts for hearing cases of violence against women, including domestic violence. Here again, we do not know what effect this discussion of family violence in public is having on the power relationships in the home. In many of the MS districts, widows now wear *bindi*, jewelry, and bright clothes. What effect this has had on their status in the home, we do not know. How does empowerment in the home happen? We are only now beginning to do research on this question.

The emerging trends throw up more questions than answers. Is empowerment measurable? Is there such a thing as being fully empowered? And is there a point in the process of empowerment when it becomes self-perpetuating? Does the means to empowerment differ according to class, status, circumstance? For example, the Sahayogini is less dependent on collective action for enhancing her self-image than the Sangha woman is. At the district, state and national levels, MS associates have recourse to several fora (groups) to meet the needs of self-growth.

These and related questions are of immediate concern in the plotting of activities for the future. The latter is expected of planned development programmes. But given that the MS is a programme for social change and that empowerment is not a package deal, with a neat beginning and end (like digging a well or building a house), its future action is not so easy to visualize.

The Sangha has been largely successful in enabling poor rural women to initiate their journey to empowerment. But their experiences with *panchayats*, savings groups, and income generating activities, highlight the tenuous link between individual empowerment and collective power. The Mahila Samakhya Programme assigns value to collective power and remains somewhat ambiguous in its reaction to individual empowerment. But even within the framework of the MS philosophy for progression in the process of empowerment, a dynamic combination of individual empowerment and collective power is called for. Collective power is essential for attempting planned and visible social change, but without individual empowerment, collective power can become authoritarian and oppressive.

Mahila Samakhya addresses social change via new equations in gender relations. This means a change in both individuals and social institutions through continuing interaction between the two.

It is not easy to provide the soil for growth without defining the furrows. There is pressure from national and international "development makers" for quick yields with short-term inputs. Roads and water, loans, pensions, and buffaloes are the cosmetics of change. It is *how* these resource are acquired, the "learning to fish" part of it, that is critical to basic and sustained social change. Will Mahila Samakhya be able to make for itself the time and space required for facilitating the internalization of the HOW of learning?

EVALUATION

Since 1989, Mahila Samakhya has undergone innumerable evaluations. There have been many internal evaluations at the state level, as well as formal joint evaluations at regular intervals for the funders (the Government of India and the Dutch Government).

PARAMETERS AND INDICATORS

Various parameters and indicators for evaluation have been worked out and modified from time to time. One such list is given below.

I. Theoretical and Operational Understanding of Concept of Sangha and Women Leadership Role

    A. Sangha

        1. Sangha definition

        2. aspects of Sangha

        3. Sangha-building

    B. Sakhi/Sahayogini

II. Content of the Programme

    A. distribution between "issue" and "activity"

    B. activities and issues taken up so far

    C. statistics of above

    D. impact of activities/issues at village level

    E. trainings/camps/meetings/celebrations

    F. implementation of the issue/activity

    G. factors affecting issue/activity

III. Access to Resources

    A. access to government schemes and other resources from outside

    B. access to resources from within the programme

IV. Interaction with Power Structures and Institutions

    A. nature of interaction at different levels—family, village, etc.

    B. frequency of interaction with outsiders

    C. impact of such interactions at the Sangha level

V. Visibility
- A. at the personal level
- B. visibility of group at village level
- C. visibility of programme to outsiders

VI. Resource Creation
- A. information/knowledge.
- B. physical resources (e.g., Sangha hut)
- C. human resources
- D. financial resources

VII. Training
- A. statistics
- B. philosophy of training
- C. trainees
- D. trainers
- E. impact of training
- F. documentation of training processes and inputs

VIII. Documentation

IX. Expansion and Growth
- A. sangha level
- B. programme level
- C. involvement in unplanned creative activities and processes
- D. role of MS in women's movement in State
- E. changes in roles
- F. phasing out

X. Programme Structures
- A. at different levels
- B. administration
- C. openness of structure
- D. intra- and inter-structural relations
- E. evaluation of roles of individuals: resource persons/administrative staff, etc.

XI. Democratization and Decentralization

    A. decision making

    B. planning strategies

    C. selection and recruitment

    D. fora

XII. Financial Management

XIII. Environment

    A. Internal

        1. relationships

        2. culture/ethos of the organization

    B. External

        1. village level

        2. with power structures

        3. with outsiders

XIV. Risks/Opportunities

    A. Internal

    B. External

XV. Demands/Pressures

XVI. Areas of Weakness/Neglect

XVII. Areas of Anxiety.

Each of the parameters is further detailed into indicators. For example:

1) *SANGHA DEFINITON*

    number of women actively and continuously involved in the process.

    number of women who join for activities only

    number of women who attend the meeting

    number of women who have undergone training

    number of outside visits by individual groups

    frequency places and time of Sangha meeting

2) *ASPECTS OF SANGHA*

    heterogeneity and openness of Sangha

    issues discussed by the Sangha

    sakhi selection processes

    leadership in the Sangha and degree of democratization of leadership roles

    facilitation of Sangha meetings

    prioritization of the issues by Sangha women

    range of issues addressed in a particular Sangha and involvement of Sangha women with the issue

    undertaking of responsibility by Sangha women and conflict handling

    decision-making process in the Sangha

    independence of the group

    affinity/identification with the ideology/group

    perception of Sangha women of Sakhi honorarium

3) *SANGHA BUILDING*

    relationship among the group members and relationship of Sangha women with other women in the village

    processes that have gone into the issue

    outside support to Sangha women (family, community, power groups, etc.)

    outsiders resorting to Sangha for support

    role of Sahayogini and Sakhi

    success or failure of activity (from the view of Sangha women)

    effect of Sakhi rotation on Sangha

    economic activities taken up by the group (and its effect on Sangha building)

    support of one Sangha by another Sangha

    financial provision for the Sangha

Some of the indicators are quantifiable; others, such as the decision-making process in the Sangha, are not. The Sahayoginis have also come up with a list of qualities of "strong" Sanghas, as follows:

- takes initiative in identifying a common cause
- responds with sensitivity to issues of exploitation/violence against women
- integrates community concerns in its agenda
- takes a decision without guidance from Sahayogini
- builds an image of "a power to reckon with" at the community level
- exerts pressure on the existing system for greater accountability to people
- attracts and sustains participation from different sets of women and men over varied issues
- holds regular meetings in which women take active interest and indulge in creative, open-minded problem solving
- encourages alternative forms of learning
- provides leadership opportunities to a greater numbers of women.

Some of the indicators are not difficult to capture because they are quantifiable (e.g., the number of women attending Sangha meetings or how many government schemes they have accessed). But even here, the main indicator is really the *how*—the process by which a particular resource is accessed. For example, was it the Sahayogini or one particular Sangha member who masterminded the activity, and the rest simply followed? There is more "empowerment" if many women participated in the discussion and in the action to acquire a specific resource.

The more difficult indicators are the qualitative ones such as facilitation of Sangha meetings, or even the impact of training. The latter can be intangible.

Another level of difficulty is when we (the evaluators, the implementers) and they (the participating women) think differently about what constitutes empowerment. For example, for us a theoretical/conceptual understanding of MS is an important indicator of empowerment. On the other hand, the women, including Sahayoginis, are not conceptually inclined. They deal with "cases" and communicate in "stories". It is the evaluators who bind a number of cases and stories into concepts. Is it necessary for everyone in the programme to do so? After all, it would appear that the spirit behind tackling the case is what matters, and if that is internalized, what does concept matter?

Another level of difficulty in evaluation is when values differ. In the study of the family, many women said they felt "strong" from wearing the same sort of clothes and eating the same sort of food as the upper caste women. For us, this is "Sanskritization" (an imitation of upper caste habits) and therefore not of intrinsic value in raising self-esteem. (Women should be proud of their own culture' and not rise through imitation.) So, how to interpret the indicator? In the course of "studying" Mahila Samakhya, it became clear to us that the rural women are not as individualistic as urban, westernized women. For them, the "Self" includes family. Often they do things to save the husband's "face", which is part of the family "face". Is becoming more individualistic rather than group-minded becoming more "empowered"? Also, by and large, the women negotiate rather than confront. Is negotiating more specially a woman's way and therefore to be more valued than confronting? Is confronting merely being imitative?

Apart from the difficulties of evaluating process and the qualitative indicators, there is the question of how "empowerment" is understood. We who study/evaluate and they who are being studied/evaluated have different worldviews. Where is the meeting point? What the compromise? How do we balance the two?

METHODOLOGY

The usual methods of evaluation were used—analysis of secondary data, interview guides, group discussions, and small group interviews. We also used case studies and 'stories' as narrated in this paper.

In the ongoing study of empowerment in the family, we have made extensive use of enactments and role play to get at undeclared/unacknowledged attitudes as well as at the texture of changing relationships. For example, in discussion, women said that if their married daughters returned home from an unhappy marriage, they would take them back into the home. In enactments, it was quite clear that pressure would be brought to bear on the daughter to return to her in-laws.

Again, when we asked women to enact what had happened at home when they went to their first MS meeting (some seven years back) and now at this present meeting (1999), little details of the interaction between husband and wife, which had not been acknowledged] in the narration, came through.

The study of the family has only recently begun, but it confirms the many complex layers of what is understood as "empowerment" by the different -groups of women engaged in this exercise of empowering themselves and others. "Evaluation" seems to connote a single-point, non-controversial, judgmental exercise, and appears to be too simplistic a tool for understanding something as complex and culturally layered as "empowerment".

Acknowledgements

This paper is a bringing together of the thoughts and actions of the thousands of women who are part of the Mahila Samakhya (Education for Women's Equality) Programme. I have interacted with many of them and I would like to thank them all for the exciting learning experience and the opportunity for growth given to me by my involvement in the programme.

My special thanks to Ms. Sharada Jain, who was my colleague in the study of Sanghas (women's collectives) that we both carried out in 1996. Also to Ms. Anjali Dave, with whom I am currently engaged in a study called, "The Home and the World," in Mahila Samakhya areas.

EVALUATION IN FEMINIST PROJECTS

Beata Fiszer

I represent a feminist organisation called PSF (Polish Feminist Association) Women's Center. Although formally established only in the latter half of 1995, PSF was actually started in 1989 as an informal group.

The Foundation runs an educational center for women in Warsaw, Poland. It organises training courses, discussion meetings, seminars, conferences, and campaigns for the rights of women (including the legalization of abortion and the elimination of discrimination and violence against women).

The Foundation also has a feminist library and archives. However, we do not like to be labelled as a "resource center." Rather, we prefer to be identified as a women's center, a place for women from which feminist politics espousing equality and emancipation can be advanced.

We have deliberately chosen to work only with women, although our publications, media campaigns and other work do reach the general public. The decision to focus our educational work exclusively on women is based on the fact that women have less access to a wide range of training courses (financial obstacles), as well as on the need to activate and develop the managerial skills of women. The long experience of the feminist movement makes it clear that men dominate in mixed groups, while the women tend to become passive, anxious and/or uncertain, and unable to reveal their needs. In this situation, education has the features of "positive discrimination".

Many groups that identify themselves as feminist or women-centred have concrete projects, many of which are sponsored by western organisations. Such projects have structures and procedures that are set by the sponsoring agency. Often, the sponsors are the ones who define the ways of reporting the course of the project, providing ready-made schemes and questionnaires for the purpose. Such reports are limited only to the presentation of the results, usually using quantitative indicators (for example, the number of organised training courses), and confirmation of the proper spending of the allotted financial resources. They are not evaluation reports.

Evaluation is a process that should be integral to the group's activity. An ideal seems to be formative evaluation, embraced from the very beginning by the project and following it while simultaneously introducing changes and renewing the organisation's sense of mission.

Carrying out evaluation effectively requires time and the involvement of the team, even if it is run by an expert from outside (in which case, it could be costly). Our organisation prefers a way of democratic evaluation which, as the name suggests, requires the participation of all, including the women who participate in our programs.

In this mode of evaluation, dialogue is central. All statements are respected. Being the subjects and the proponents of the evaluation at the same time, we inevitably introduce our own hierarchies of values and ways of thinking, especially because the organisation has a very strong ideological basis.

When evaluating the extent to which the organisation's goals have been achieved, we come across certain difficulties. The goals of a feminist group are generally long-term, very difficult to measure social objectives—e.g., to change attitudes toward violence against women. It sometimes happens that objectives of this kind obscure others which are the project's aims, being in reality the means of attaining those hidden ones (e.g., the hidden objective is quality change of political institutions like Parliament, while the project aim is increasing the number of women deputies through political education of women).

In this regard, it is important to prepare appropriate indicators of quality, especially the quality of a change.

Feminist organisations in Poland have to contend with very unfavourable conditions. The government has completely given up implementing the Platform for Action formulated in Beijing in 1995 and Parliament has rejected the Equal Rights Bill. Projects counteracting domestic violence have been abandoned because of the mistaken notion that they are an attack against the family. The Catholic Church supports conservative tendencies and the traditional division of the roles of men and women. Abortion and sterilisation are illegal. Even where there is a valid reason to terminate a pregnancy, the public health service makes it as difficult as possible for women to have an abortion.

Despite all these, it is very difficult to get funds from western sponsors. The latter tend to think that the situation in Poland is becoming normal, that democracy is getting stronger, and that support for NGOs is no longer as necessary as it was during the transformation stage.

Another phenomenon is a tendency on the part of individuals and institutions that have a positive attitude to women's issues, to focus the activities of women's organisations on situations requiring immediate assistance for those in need. Refraining from direct involvement is criticized and is considered an inability to transform "egg-head theory" into practice.

We are expected to provide services rather than work out system solutions. However, this expectation conforms to or acquieses with the stereotype of a woman sacrificing herself for others. Central to feminist politics is the transformation of the system. Every feminist project should assume that even as a distant goal. And it is an emotional experience for an organisation to realise that its activities do not implement any quality changes but instead strengthen the system that generates the pathology the organisation seeks to address in the first place.

A good example is a founder of a shelter for battered women in Germany who, after many years of work in the shelter, found from her analysis of the wider social context that the perpetrators are still unpunished. In Germany, there are hardly any convictions for cruelty to spouses; no procedures have been introduced which would punish the perpetrators. It is still a woman and her children who have to abandon their home in domestic violence situations. Many people think that since there are shelters, the problem of domestic violence has been solved. What the founder of such a shelter realized is that an issue she had wanted to make public had suddenly "disappeared", so that even the neighbours of battered women no longer recognise them and the victims of the most cruel acts of violence return to their "butchers".

This woman, whom I interviewed, said that while she and her shelter had been sponsored for years by the state, she was at the same time used by the system to separate victims and channel their various needs into one—the need for "emergency" safety. She felt that although she could provide me with a long list of victims who were offered help and the shelter was expanding and was better equipped and managed than in the beginning, the goal in this social field had not been achieved.

What is evident here is that the criterion "R", which stands for "realism" in the SMART construction, was not part of my interlocutor's evaluation mechanism. The fact is that many women and children were saved from being battered. This cannot be overlooked.

This example shows how profound analysis should be applied to the anticipated and real results of an activity in order to succeed or at least not to suffer from deep frustration.

In this regard, the category of a goal for a feminist organisation is important. It is also important to introduce the project's goal into the sponsor's general evaluation policy. There must be agreement or consensus on the level of declared values of both the organisation and its sponsors.

But because achieving this kind of unanimity is very difficult, [the relationship between the feminist organisation and its sponsor] may sometimes be reduced to the question of how to stay a virgin and take the money. This is a case of a thoroughly instrumental treatment of the sponsor, where the paramount of concern is how to maintain the organisation's autonomy.

At the same time, we notice that groups oriented only to "spending" grants (groups that have neither their own preferences nor vision; they can do every project for which money or funding is available) are being established. For such organisations, what is important is survival, ensuring continuity of employment, or maintaining tangible assets (a place, equipment etc.). Groups of this type carry out an intensive promotion of achieved results; they boast about their quantity indicators and are not willing to talk about mission.

They are not alone in this respect. From our experience and that of other groups, and as discussed by German feminist Marie Sichtermann, after many years of work requiring great emotional involvement and sacrifice, going through many conflicts, and suffering many failures, the primal mission is becoming a taboo. The women are afraid to come back to it because they want to keep the integrity of the group. Of course, sticking to an illusory feeling of community may result in the negation of the most essential values of the organisation or movement; it may cause a sense of frustration, destroy real bonds, and induce paralysis.

My own organisation has undergone all the stages of team formation. After the last crisis, which was also a conflict of values, it entered a new phase of reform.

It was easier to apply creative solutions to long drawn-out conflicts, with the assistance of an expert from outside the organisation, a person whom we had known for a long time and who had a positive attitude toward our organisation. Choosing this person raised the sense of security, and nobody felt that she was being evaluated or exposed to danger. An additional impulse of the evaluation was the fact that the expert worked for us voluntarily. [This bears stressing because] in fact there is no possibility of introducing a budget item called "evaluation report" even though we are forced by our sponsors to have evaluation reports prepared by chartered accountants. From a utilitarian point of view, auditing is a positive phenomenon because with it the organisation's credibility and prestige with the sponsoring agency increases. But from the point of view of the everyday needs of a project, instead of a chartered accountant, a good bookkeeping firm or accountant is needed. Unfortunately, the sponsors provide for the latter with great reluctance. Insufficient financing of infrastructure is a problem that majority of organisations cope with; it in turn adversely affects the merits of the organisation's work. Maybe this is a case of needing too much money to implement projects (merit is overblown to cover up structural needs). Over-calculating [financial resources] may be a result of lack of up-to-date monitoring or the inability to recognise one's own resources (including human resources), abilities, and needs.

In our evaluation, the culture of the organisation was skillfully reconstructed; the structure of decision making was analysed; and competencies, ways of communicating, and the organisation's mission were revalued.

By working together, we managed to separate the facts about our functioning from individual interpretations. Equally important was that everything related to the evaluation process used. As a team we learned a lot and in our everyday practice we have developed many valuable managerial skills. We took part in many training courses (including team building, negotiating), which we are able to use and which we can now conduct as trainers ourselves. Paradoxically, in an educational project we ran, the training of the team itself was not taken into account. In accordance with the project's assumptions, the leaders of the organisation were to become clerks. This is one of the main threats to social movements: what I call "pacification" of the leaders.

Understanding the inadequacies of the project's structure for our goals allowed us to introduce necessary changes (a course on the management of change was one of the training courses in which we took part as a team). Everything went as in a classical evaluation spiral. Projects that, as I mentioned in the beginning, have a very rigidly defined merit framework and a fixed budget, surrender to verification with some difficulties. Sometimes the sponsors themselves are interested in it because they do not want additional work, which range from reading reports to introducing changes. If the changes are radical and they involve reorganisation of the financial structure, the approval of the sponsor is necessary. Here there are established procedures which, in general, are time consuming. And it may happen that we do not have enough time to implement changes and we are forced to run the project on the basis of old assumptions and procedures to keep up with the project's schedule. We are left with the results of our evaluation in mid-air, we feel frustrated, a lot of positive energy has been wasted.

Taking into account evaluation from the very beginning of the project would allow more flexibility into the projects and will have a favourable impact on their dynamics. Perhaps this will become the rule soon because fixed procedures of the ISO type are being introduced.

Besides evaluating the system globally, we evaluate particular parts of our activity. For example, in the educational field, when we work with the materials from outside, or those not prepared by us—this is something that happens often because we hire professional training organisations, we evaluate the training materials from the point of view of their usefulness and appropriateness for women. We have found that the majority of the manuals are directed to a male recipient, they are written in masculine gender and the illustrations depict only men. And the majority of trainers' examples do not relate to the women's experiences. When we want to address our training to our clients, everything must change, including the language used. Any appearance of gender discriminatory (or of other similar categories) content is inadmissible. The issue of icebreakers based on jokes should be pointed out here. [The jokes should not be at the expense of women.] Also, the trainers must be women. Not all firms will fulfill this condition.

We stick to these assumptions when we ourselves prepare our own workshops. The latter are still far too scarce, and they are experimental in nature because too much time is needed to prepare a workshop and we need to be able to harmonise this activity with the needs of the Center. Still, we hope that in a project being planned right now it will be one of the priorities. After the training course, the participants should be given the evaluation questionnaires. Even when the activities are run by external trainers, this step is not neglected so that we get an insight into the source material and possibly a report.

I must admit that when the workshops are run by our team, we often fail to apply this procedure. We are well theoretically prepared for using an evaluating questionnaire: we are also aware that in order to "heighten" the valuation, it is necessary to do a round table discussion on the training with the participants before asking them to fill out the questionnaire. Then they can be sent one more questionnaire to be filled out "soberly." But so far, we have not been able to work out a satisfying questionnaire. When we use a typical questionnaire we get feedback that there is too much formality, the form is dull etc. We wonder how to construct a tool more attractive for women, which at the same time would possess methodological correctness and be functional.

In closing, I would like to share with you my experience with evaluation results which at first seemed to undermine our very existence but which, after we had analysed them, turned out to be very stimulating.

Last year we started to notice a decline in our clients' interest in so-called political issues and activities, as well as a considerable increase in activity in the fields which we considered "by-products" of our Foundation. This phenomenon was worth a deeper consideration. For this, we decided to choose the focus group interview method. Moderators from outside the Center talked with the women about their preferences, needs, situation, and visions as regards the Center and groups related to it in the new 21st century.

The result was the following: the women, who had been trained by us and who had actively supported various political actions such as those for the Equal Status of Women and Men Law, expressed their deep aversion to and disillusionment with what they called institutional politics. They maintained their eagerness to, above all, maintain their bonds with other women because of shared values and empowerment. They strongly emphasised the need for spaces for women which could be safe places for intellectual and emotional stimulation. The expression most often used was: "we want to meet with each other."

For some time, we were unable to find the key to understanding what lies behind this sentence because we did not have an adequate language for the description of this situation. In analytical work, we tried to walk away from political categories used until then, such as discrimination, political representation, and gender-based violence, and to find an original value. We agreed that this original value for us is freedom. This is the fundamental category for our organisation.

To translate freedom into practical action, we decided to organise a conference dedicated to women's freedom although earlier we had planned a session directly related to the 50th anniversary of the International Bill of Human Rights. The key figures of our conference were representatives of Libreria delle Donne di Milano, whom we contacted through the German feminists (in Poland there is no feminist literature). The concept of women's freedom presented by them—the politics of relationships and desires—was met with an enthusiastic response from the Polish participants. The conference was held at the end of November and from the beginning of December, there have been regular discussion meetings dedicated to the Italian women's philosophy at the Center.

Right now, our organisation is going through a very intellectually prolific stage. It is noticeable that postulated assumptions of the politics of relationships have had an influence on relations inside our group and outside it. The path of desire has turned out to be very appealing to the women.

Still searching for feedback related to our activity, through quality techniques (FGI and deepened interview) we have found out that the women need the Centre to:

- construct educational projects and workshops;
- train women (including political leaders) in women's issues;
- train women in skills that are helpful to their professional and social life ;
- work with small groups of women;
- get inspiration and self-fulfilment
- learn from women from other countries;
- collect data, make researches, and analyse them;
- create a "map of women's situation";
- work on language and women's perspective;

- prepare methods and tools;
- draw up reports;
- create women's politics;
- publish women's magazine, books, materials;
- create new spaces for women;
- build new projects;
- create culture and cooperation with women at the local level;
- create equal educational opportunities for women and men by making offers accessible and addressing them to women.

The knowledge we gained helped us to construct the Center of Feminist Politics, a new project which our Foundation is going to implement in the coming years.

PART 3
Monitoring International Commitments

EVALUATING NGO WORK IN EDUCATION FOR ALL FROM A GENDER PERSPECTIVE

Berewa Jommo

Conceptual Framework for the Evaluation

Gender in basic education, both formal and non-formal, is about more than putting girls into schools or women into literacy programmes. We need to look at how learning institutions and their environments prepare girls and women to overcome oppressive gender roles and to transform their lives and their communities. Gender programmes are about promoting changes in the relations between women and men, girls and boys to help them make more conscious choices about their roles in society. Gender programmes are about power sharing.

The following guidelines are intended to help NGOs assess the gender dimensions of their basic literacy, non-formal and formal education work. At a general level, the objective of the evaluation exercise is to gain a better understanding of how NGO policies in basic formal and non-formal education have changed over the past ten years, specifically in the area of gender mainstreaming[1], and what the underlying processes and mechanisms are in putting these policies into practice. Concretely, we require information on a broad spectrum of basic education activities that promote gender equity. Here again the analysis of processes underlying these activities are of particular interest in understanding the degree of success or failure of a particular activity and in drawing conclusions for the future.

Guidelines for the Gender Analysis

The following five-point guideline, partly framed in the form of questions, is meant to help NGOs to analyse and assess their work in gender in basic education. Information should be given in summaries not exceeding one page per question.

I. General Policy Context: Conducive to Gender Programmes in Basic Education?

> The following analysis will allow for a better understanding of whether the general gender policies providing the context of your NGO's work are conducive, indifferent, complementary and/or contradictory to your efforts in gender and basic education.

Give a brief analysis of the overall shifts in gender policies in basic education over the past ten years which form the context of your NGO's activities.

II. NGO Gender Policies and Basic Education: Shifts or Stagnation?

> The following policy description and analysis will allow you to assess how far your NGO has incorporated the gender dimension both internally, within your organisation, and in your basic education programmes. The questions asked should help you analyse your organisation's performance in areas II a) and b). However, these questions are only "pointers" and are not meant to be exhaustive. There is therefore room for improvement and/or responses to additional questions which may be generated by your analysis.

a) Describe the shifts in organisational policies with regard to gender that your NGO has been undergoing over the past ten years.

Does your organisation have a gender code of conduct?
What was the process by which this gender code of conduct was developed?

b) Describe the processes, structures and mechanisms for gender mainstreaming (conceptualising, planning, implementing, monitoring, evaluating) in your NGO's basic education programmes.

To what extent do your training policies prepare your staff/educators (resource people, teachers, trainers, facilitators, etc.) to facilitate gender sensitive learning?

How do you go about developing gender sensitive content areas and learning materials for your programmes?

In what way do traditional women's knowledge/learning systems form part of your learning programmes?

How do you ensure that the learning taking place in your programmes contributes to educating responsible members, both women and men, of the family, community, and society as a whole?

To what extent do your programmes promote access to and retention in basic education programmes, formal and/or non formal, for girls and women?

How do you monitor and evaluate your programmes from a gender perspective?

III. IMPACT ON GENDER EQUITY AND WOMEN'S EMPOWERMENT

> The examples you are asked to give in the following will allow you to assess how you have contributed to promote the empowerment of women and other gender relevant changes in society in general, and in basic education in particular.

a) Give specific examples of how your NGO's interventions in Education for All have resulted in shifts in gender attitudes, habits and behaviours with regard to the basic education of girls and women.

b) Give concrete examples of the impact of your interventions on the empowerment of women and on gender relations.

IV. LEARNING FROM DIFFICULT EXPERIENCES

Give examples of obstacles you encountered in making or trying to make gender equity a reality in your basic education programmes. What measures did you take to overcome these obstacles?

What lessons have you learned from overcoming or not being able to overcome obstacles to integrating the gender dimension in your work?

V. LOOKING TO THE FUTURE

From the above analysis, what conclusions can you draw about the prospects of gender equity in basic education in general, and in your organisation in particular? Formulate recommendations for gender mainstreaming in life long learning in Education for All.

Notes

[1] The term "gender mainstreaming" refers to the degree to which gender sensitivity, balance and equity are incorporated in given policies, programmes and practices.

WOMEN PARTICIPATION: BRIDGING THE GAP

Celita Eccher

Since the early 1990's, women have been involved in the UN Conferences, which increased awareness of certain issues that until then were not part of the global debate. This Social Cycle of Conferences made apparent two developments which I would like to highlight. First, the emergence of a global vision of things. The state and civil society organisations gathered to discuss issues such as education, environment, human rights, poverty, population and social development. The Fourth World Conference on Women (WCW) in Beijing was a major step forward. Second, the improvement of NGOs' capacity to monitor and intervene in conferences since Eco-Rio, particularly in women capacity-building as was beautifully symbolised by Femea Planet.

Women's caucuses have become a remarkable participatory tool and have proven to be an excellent exercise of women's global citizenship. This exercise has been accompanied by constant and stubborn political pressure to broaden and better understand women's citizenship, defined as the right to have rights and to exercise them.

Furthermore, and quoting Gita Sen, "Globalisation requires actions at global level... International Conferences have become important events and arenas in which feminist organisations have to struggle against patriarchal forces. Globalisation offers new spaces in which new demands can be presented and global commitments can be assumed. But local demands and local ways of mobilisation must persist..." (Sen, 1998). Given this global context, many women around the world have begun to recognize the importance of learning and participating at both the global and the local level. In other words, women have to be everywhere. Some of us must work at the local level and others at the global level. The challenge is to create linkages between these two levels; that is to say, to improve our capacity for articulation.

"Participation at the global level proved to be a good exercise of human rights, in which the world women's movement has had the chance to raise its voice, ask for accountability and monitor the actions of governments as they relate to the recommendations assumed in the Conferences.

In this global context, some civil society organisations have been forced to evaluate and modify their strategies and actions that until then had not considered the articulation with the state and other international organisms.

I believe that the most important change in civil society organizations' approach is the interest in intervening in governmental and inter-governmental decisions. This implies a movement towards negotiation and sharper articulation"(Bonino & Eccher).

This new vision requires NGO capacity-building, sharper articulation, and above all, the creation of alliances and linkages for negotiation. We have learned that we walk the same path, backwards and forward.

However, the relevance of intervening at Conferences and influencing decision-making is still being debated among NGOs. I am the co-ordinator of two networks and I would like to share with you our experiences in this respect.

The Popular Education Network of Women (REPEM), an active regional network in Latin America and the Caribbean specialising in women's adult education, participated in preparatory events for the International Conferences. REPEM also committed to follow up, through its own programme on poverty and education, the Social Summit, Fourth WCW Platform of Action and CONFINTEA V Recommendations as they relate to education, gender, and poverty. REPEM's programmes strive to improve the situation of grassroots women in the region and foster their participation through the exercise of their rights.

REPEM supports the Gender and Education Office (GEO) of ICAE based in Uruguay. GEO's programmes aim at promoting gender-oriented education. Formerly, the ICAE Women's Programme, acted as an international network linking women, organisations and educators working with grassroots women from all over the world. At the NGO Forum of the World Conference on Women in Beijing, ICAE's Women's programme organised a workshop on the role men play in the education of women. The participants concluded that there was a need to educate both men and women about oppression, equality, marginalisation, empowerment, changing gender roles, and the rigidity of patriarchal structures.

Given this inclusive perspective, the need to introduce a new approach to the problem emerged. On the eve of a new century, the ICAE elaborated a strategic plan called,

"A Seven-Year Plan for Major Institutional Change." REPEM-CEAAL proposed the creation of the Gender and Education Office within ICAE's new seven-year plan, and after some consultation the Women's Programme became the Gender and Education Office.

GEO's main aim is to highlight and analyse the educational dimension through gender-oriented activities. GEO promotes the use of political pressure on and lobby with the state and civil society organisations about public policy, reproductive rights, democracy, and communication in order to reach a more comprehensive approach to women's adult education.

In light of its principal mission, GEO committed itself to preparations for CONFINTEA V. This was made possible thanks to the support of REPEM, which maintains strong ties with the women's movement. As a result of this collaboration, GEO was able to convoke a large group of women every morning at the Women's CAUCUS at CONFINTEA V to formulate political strategies and prepare the amendments to the documents.

As a follow-up to CONFINTEA V, GEO began work on a proposal for collecting data in several countries in Latin America, Africa, Asia, and Europe for the Index of Accomplished Commitments on Gender and Education developed by REPEM. GEO and various women's NGOs in the different regions co-organised regional meetings to present the proposal and to discuss strategies for its implementation. To date, we have more than one country study per region, and these will be published and distributed in the form of regional booklets by May 1999. Some of you have been actively involved in GEO's programme of "learning gender justice". Through these regional meetings we hope to identify other groups and individuals in Latin America, Africa, Asia, and Europe whom we hope will also work with GEO.

LATIN AMERICA

The first follow-up meeting was held from June 22 to 25, 1998 in Santa Cruz de la Sierra, Bolivia, and hosted by REPEM. Forty women from twelve different countries—Argentina, Brazil, Bolivia, Colombia, Chile, Ecuador, Dominican Republic, Mexico, Uruguay, Venezuela, Canada and the United States—discussed how to improve their political pressure skills and how to contribute to the initiatives of Educational Watch. Five women from Bolivia, Brazil, Chile, Mexico, and Uruguay, who had worked on the indicators on gender and women's adult education at the national level, are disseminating the results of this meeting. This year's edition of Social Watch published these results in its 1999 edition, representing another avenue of co-ordination and collaboration.

AFRICA

The meeting in Africa was organised by GEO together with the Adults Educators and Trainers Association of South Africa and the German Association for Adult Education or DVV, and was held from August 30 to September 2, 1998 in Cape Town, South Africa. A total of 29 women attended from 7 African countries: Botswana, Zimbabwe, Kenya, Senegal, Uganda, Zambia, and South Africa. The Index of Accomplished Commitments on Gender and Adult Education. developed by REPEM in Latin America was adopted and adapted at the Cape Town. Representatives from Zambia and South Africa worked to elaborate the political indicators in the Index.

ASIA

The meeting in Asia was organised by GEO together with the Asian South Pacific Bureau for Adult Education. It was held from September 26 to 27, 1998 in Thailand. A total of 17 participants from women's education groups in the following countries attended the meeting. Thailand, Philippines, Fiji, Solomon Islands, Indonesia, Sri Lanka, Cambodia, Hongkong SAR, Nepal, Japan, Indonesia, India, Taiwan. The proposal on the Index of Accomplished Commitments was received with a lot of enthusiasm. Through Development Alternatives with Women for the New Era or DAWN, we contacted a group of women who agreed to carry out country studies in the Philippines, Thailand, Malaysia, Indonesia, and Fiji

EUROPE

The meeting in Europe took place in Florence, Italy from November 27 to 30, 1998. It was hosted by GEO in partnership with the Commune di Firenze and the University of Firenze and with the support of UNESCO Institute of Education (UIE) in Hamburg. The REPEM Index was presented and Moldavia, Portugal, and Spain committed to presenting country studies by the end of April.

The follow-up process, according to some of the facilitators, was enhanced by:

1) the wealth of experience of the women's movement and the collective commitment to disseminating its findings;

2) the contribution and support of global networks such as DAWN, WEDO, IWTC, the Gender Unit of the UIE, and Social Watch;

3) the constant flow of ideas from the women who engaged in this process with GEO and who shared their experience and knowledge about follow-up strategies; and;

4) the women's will to learn and to exercise their citizenship in a more conscious way.

But we also faced some obstacles.

1) New proposals had to be considered in the context of less advanced institutional structures and perspectives, and this provoked some resistance and created some misunderstanding.
2) While many government representatives and NGOs recognise the importance of monitoring actions, some, particularly those who do not belong to the women's movement or any other social movement, still lack sufficient knowledge about the real significance of these actions.
3) There is a lack of resources.
4) We encountered some difficulties in the organisation.
5) There is still a lack of ability to promote alliances especially within male-dominated contexts.

As feminist activists we are aware of the importance of participating and lobbying in International Conferences. But participation should only be part of our interest. The hardest work is in monitoring the recommendations that come out of these Conferences. Since CONFINTEA V was held in Hamburg in 1997, many monitoring exercises have been conducted in order to ensure that the CONFINTEA V recommendations are being taken seriously by the different governments.

As the final stage of GEO's project, we are going to publish regional booklets that will include different monitoring experiences relevant to each region, CONFINTEA V recommendations on gender and education, and guidelines on how to implement follow-up exercises in the different regions.

Each stage of GEO's project required a lot of time and effort from both staff and collaborators to improve our monitoring exercise and affirm the need for effective follow-up actions. We are glad to say that GEO has gained recognition and strength, thanks to the precious work that we and other NGOs and individuals who share our concerns did in the different regions. The improved technological infrastructure of GEO, better communication among GEO partners, and the use of electronic mail have resulted in a continuous flow of information that enriches our work daily. We have also created a monthly electronic magazine called "Voices Rising" which features GEO's activities as well as relevant information from the different regions. Despite the strides that we have made, however, GEO is still a relatively young global network and as such its continuity depends on several factors, namely, political will, ICAE and its regional programmes' decisions, resources, and last but not least, women's creativity.

The next section describes three monitoring experiences, namely, the REPEM proposal on the Index of Accomplished Commitments on Gender and Education; the Redeh monitoring activity in Brazil; and the Network of Women of Columbia's plan, "Social Justice for Women: A Plan for the New Millennium."

SOCIAL WATCH ON EDUCATION AND GENDER: A PROPOSAL FROM REPEM

An outstanding characteristic of the recent world social conferences--from Cairo to Hamburg--has been the presence of civil society through non-governmental organisations. (NGOs) and thematic, regional and global networks. Never before have organised sectors of society had such capacity for influencing global meetings. Complementing this strong participation is another and equally new process: civil society's commitment to follow up on the agreements reached at these conferences. This follow-up implies, among other activities, monitoring fulfillment of the agreements.

Within this framework (following the line launched at the Social Summit by Social Watch), REPEM has set itself the task of monitoring some of the Social Summit agreements on education and gender equity in, initially, five Latin American five countries. While the Social Summit presented the major themes in these areas, the Fourth International Women's Conference (Beijing) refined the concepts of equity and equal opportunity in gender relationships. The UNESCO Hamburg Conference elaborated on the Beijing agreements and advanced them on more specific levels, such as 'education and adult women'.

What are we monitoring?

The fifth and sixth Copenhagen commitments provide the basis for this monitoring activity, as they cover both gender equity and the need to integrate gender equity in the educational development of the whole population.

From Commitment 5, sub-paragraphs (f) and (j)have been selected: "Establish policies, objectives and goals that enhance the equality of status, welfare and opportunity of the girl child, especially in regard to health, nutrition, literacy and education..."; and "Formulate or strengthen policies and practices to ensure that women are enabled to participate fully in paid work and in employment through such measures as positive action ..."

From Commitment 6, sub-paragraphs (c) and (g) were selected: "Ensure full and equal access to education for girls and women, recognising that investing in women's education is the key element in achieving social equality..."; and "Develop broad-based education programmes that promote and strengthen respect for all human rights and fundamental freedoms, including the right to development, promote the values of tolerance, responsibility and respect for the diversity..."

On the basis of these major principles, some specific agreements related to adult women from the UNESCO Hamburg Conference were also selected. This selection took the following criteria into account:

1) They should be representative of substantive areas regarding women's educational opportunities.
2) They should be able to be transformed into indicators.
3) Information on these agreements should be relatively accessible.

Some of the agreements selected on this basis deal with adult women's education. Others concern the governments' political will to change inequitable and unequal situations.

There are various problems with the information gathered. In the first place, since the data on situation indicators come from household censuses or continuous surveys, it has not been possible to unify all the information for the same year. In all cases, however, information was taken for the last year available. In the second place, for indicators on political will, information was not always available and monitoring criteria may not have been totally homogeneous. Where discrepancies occurred, the criteria used in each case are clarified.

Examples of two indicators monitored for 1998 in Bolivia, Brazil, Chile, Mexico, and Uruguay are given below. It is hoped not only that as these indicators evolve monitoring will continue year after year, but also that it will be extended to the whole region.

AGREEMENT: To promote the empowerment of women and gender equity through adult learning by eliminating gender disparities in access to all areas and levels of education.

Chart 1. Women of 14 years of age and over by level of education, by country (in percentages)

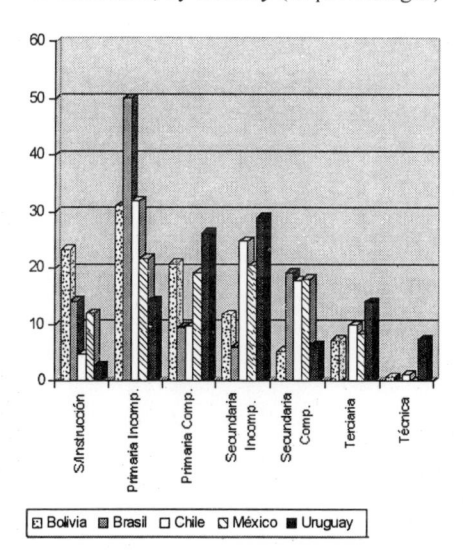

Bolivia and Brazil rate particularly low on this indicator. Over 20 percent of Bolivian women do not have any education while 30 percent have not completed primary school. Fifty percent of Brazilian women have not completed primary school while approximately 15 percent have no education. Uruguay and Chile have the highest levels. A chart with information on the total population is included for comparison (Chart 2).

Chart 2. Inequality between women and men at the different levels of education, by country (in percentages)

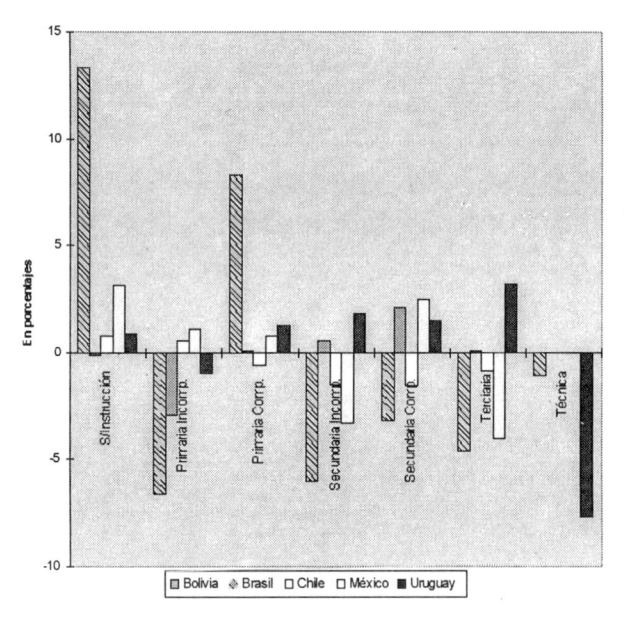

This indicator was built by comparing the level of education reached by adult men and women. Bolivia shows the highest level of inequality, with women ranking lower in all cases but one. The other countries, except Uruguay where women rank higher than men at nearly all levels, show relatively moderate levels of inequality.

BRAZIL: AN NGO IN COLLABORATION

Another monitoring experience took place in Rio de Janeiro, Brazil. It started as a project of the NGO Red de Defensa de la Especie Humana or REDEH in collaboration with the Rio de Janeiro State (REDEH, 1998). But it proved to be such an outstanding success that the Government of Brazil decided to include the proposal in the national educational syllabus and distributed one million copies to teachers nationwide.

This project was created in line with the following commitments.

In Chapter 3 of the Agenda for the Future of Adult Learning, Governments commit themselves to:

> 25b) Emphasising the importance of literacy for human rights; participatory citizenship; social and political, economic equity, and cultural identity

In Chapter 1 of the Agenda, Governments commit to:

> 13b) Taking measures to eliminate discrimination in education at all levels on the basis of gender, race, language, religion, national origin, disability, or any other form of discrimination.

The right to basic education is guaranteed in the Federal Constitution of 1998, which states that the state must facilitate citizens' access to education. Millions of Brazilians are over the regular schooling age. We therefore face the challenge of looking for the means to guarantee those people access to basic education, and enable them to participate actively in politics, culture, and the economy. Women are the most disadvantaged in the country. But since they make up a large portion of the population, and are still growing in number, they can join forces and strengthen ties with the state and other civil society groups in order to improve their situation.

Non-gender-oriented education is considered by women's movements as one of the obstacles to the creation of a more democratic society where gender justice exists. Given this, CACES, REDEH (Red de Defensa de la Especie Humana), and CEDIM (Consejo Estadual dos Direitos da Mulher do Estado de Rio de Janeiro), with support from the Secretaria de Enseflanza del Ministerio de Educacion y Deporte, have established linkages with teachers working with adolescentes and adults to discuss a gendered and non-racist educational alternative. They have put together an educational kit, consisting of audio cassettes, a video cassette, and a booklet, that raises awareness on many of the issues in women-men relationships. This kit is a useful tool in paving the way for democratic education that promotes equality among men and women of different ages and ethnical origins as well as between human beings and nature. It was created for teachers who believe in the need for transformation. Within this framework, co-operative work is a must and we call on everyone who shares our beliefs to join this project.

COLOMBIA: A PLAN FOR THE 21ST CENTURY

Each new government in Colombia is required to present to the National Council a four-year plan for discussion and approval. The National Council is represented by different social sectors including the women's movement.

The Network of Women of Colombia, which is composed of eight women's networks, presented a formal proposal to the National Council for Planning and to the Congress of Colombia in response to the Plan of the New Government of Andres Pastrana (FemPress, 1999). The objective of the Network is to introduce a gender perspective in policy-making. It prepared a 79-paged document, "Social Justice for Women: A Plan for the New Millennium," which addresses issues such gender justice, equity, and poverty, and covers the areas of health, women's participation, environment, and rural women's situation and place. It also emphasises the need for women's issues to be given special attention in the Government Plan which, in its original, lacks positive measures to overcome discriminatory practices against women.

Each member-network of the Network of Women of Colombia worked on a different section of the document according to its specific experience. REPEM-Colombia collaborated on the section on Rural Women's Situation and Place , referring to the recommendations of CONFINTEA V as they relate to education and gender to draft the amendments. The document was edited by Ana Cristina Gonzales and Cecilia Barraza. The elaboration of this document is part of the project called "Strengthening Political Action of the Women's Network as Part of the Social Movement of Women," which was made possible with the support of German Co-operation and the National Department for Equity.

This document proved to be an excellent exercise towards two key objectives. The first objective was to intervene in policy-making in order to effect structural transformation, particularly in regard to the subordination of women, while building a plan for development that fosters women empowerment, equal opportunities, and people's awareness of the role that women play in the development of their own citizenship. The second objective is to achieve full recognition of women's rights and women's contribution to national and economic development, and to peace construction To this end, the Network demands that the Plan recognise the role of women in society and commit political and economic resources to achieving equity.

WORKS CITED

Bonino, M. and Eccher, C. De lo Local a lo Global y de lo Global a lo Local, aprendizajes para una estrategia de educacion y genero.

FemPress. 1999. *Agencia de Prensa de la Mujer Latinoamericano*, Santiago de Chile.

REDEH. 1998. Ciudadania y Genero: Manual Para Alfabetizacao de Jovens e Adultos(as).

Sen, Gita. 1998. Los Desafios de la Globalización. Montevideo: REPEM-DAWN.

MONITORING EDUCATION PROGRAMMES IN PACIFIC ISLAND COUNTRIES

Margaret Chung

INTRODUCTION

This paper discusses practices of monitoring and evaluating education programmes from a macro-level perspective, that is, as part of monitoring sustainable human development in Pacific island countries. A principal problem throughout the Pacific is the rarity of data from which to analyse what is happening with adult education, especially women's education, in order to map out the linkages with other development changes and put adult education higher on the policy agenda.

The Pacific island region includes 15 separate countries, which are members or associate members of the United Nations, namely Cook Islands, Fiji Islands, Kiribati, Marshall Islands, Federated States of Micronesia, Nauru, Niue, Palau, Papua New Guinea, Samoa, Solomon Islands, Tokelau, Tonga, Tuvalu and Vanuatu. There are great differences in the size, population, resource endowment, and environmental condition of these countries. There is also a great deal of difference in their human development status. In most of the smaller Polynesian island countries, high quality education for children is now almost universal. In the Melanesian countries of Vanuatu, Solomon Islands and Papua New Guinea, providing children access to elementary education is still a major policy concern while adult education receives much less attention.

Yet throughout the region, a most urgent issue confronting policymakers is how to ensure that all people have secure, sustainable livelihood, livelihood that meets their aspirations and needs. While in the past the majority of Pacific island people were subsistence farmers, this situation is rapidly changing. Even in the remotest parts of the region, most households need some cash income. The formal job sector caters to only a minority of workers. Economic and demographic trends suggest that the gap between the demand for and the availability of paid employment will almost certainly grow. The challenge is to both generate employment in the modern sector and increase labour absorption and productivity in the informal sector.

Adult education is necessary not just to help create these livelihood opportunities, but to promote human development in many other aspects, including self-fulfillment and fuller participation in economic and political processes. Yet adult education, non-formal education in particular, receives very little policy attention or resources in this region of the world. It is largely ad hoc in its organization and is seen by governments as the domain of NGOs. Governments view education programmes principally as formal education for children. In order to get adult education, particularly women's education, firmly onto the policy agenda, more needs to be known about the nature and status of these programmes, and how they contribute to overall development processes. That is where quite elementary, baseline statistics come in, and where our inability in the Pacific to accurately estimate such things as adult literacy and programme participation rates are real impediments to change.

ADULT LITERACY

Adult literacy is a basic measure of development status, and is a component of the UNDP Human Development Index. Actual survey data is available for very few Pacific island countries, the most recent survey being in the Solomon Islands in 1991 (which found only 23 percent of women to be literate). Figures are often cited in official documents, but their basis is quite uncertain. In fact, they are little more than guesses and, judging by the number of countries that officially report close to 100 percent adult literacy, hopeful guesses at that. In order to have a comparable measure across the region, the recent UNDP Human Development Report used the conventional census-based proxy

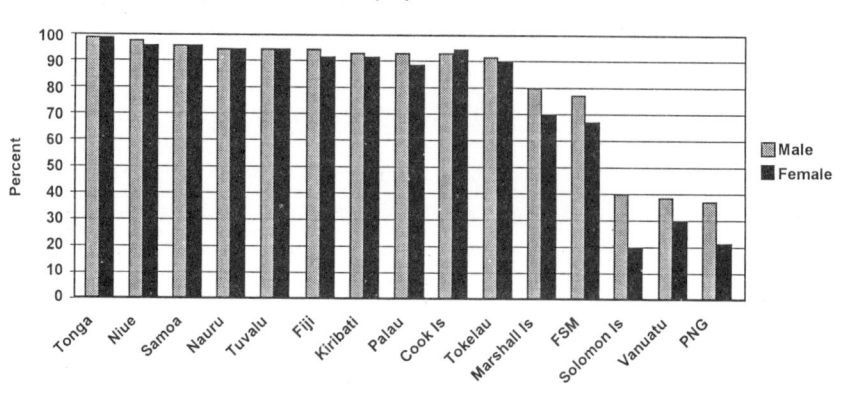

Figure 1. Adult Literacy, by sex, in Pacific island countries

of the proportion of adults aged 15 years and older who had less than four years of formal education. As Figure 1 shows, the gap between men's and women's literacy widens as overall literacy falls. Although the statistics used in Figure 1 are mostly lower than the official figures usually quoted, Figure 1 is probably still quite an overestimation of functional literacy. Especially among older adults who once attended rural schools, literacy is not a much practiced skill, other than perhaps for reading the Bible.

GROSS ENROLMENT RATIOS

Gross enrolment ratios, another basic development indicator, measure the proportion of children and young people aged five to 24 years enroled in school. The "Pacific Island Countries' Human Development Report 1999" limited the calculation of the gross enrolment ratio to five to 19 year olds, as most Pacific island countries do not have tertiary institutions and most of the few students who reach this level study abroad (UNDP, 1999). Inclusion of the older age group, 20 to 24, would therefore have substantially deflated the gross enrolment ratio for these countries.

Gross enrolment ratios are indicative of the need for basic adult education, and non-formal education in general, in that in their inverse they show the proportion of children who are not in school. Moreover, gross enrolment ratios across the Pacific shown in Figure 2 are closely correlated to adult literacy statistics shown in Figure 1, demonstrating the real need for non-formal basic education programmes in some Pacific island countries. The gender gap in the gross enrolment ratio is less than in adult literacy. This shows that more young women today have access to school than previous generations of girls.

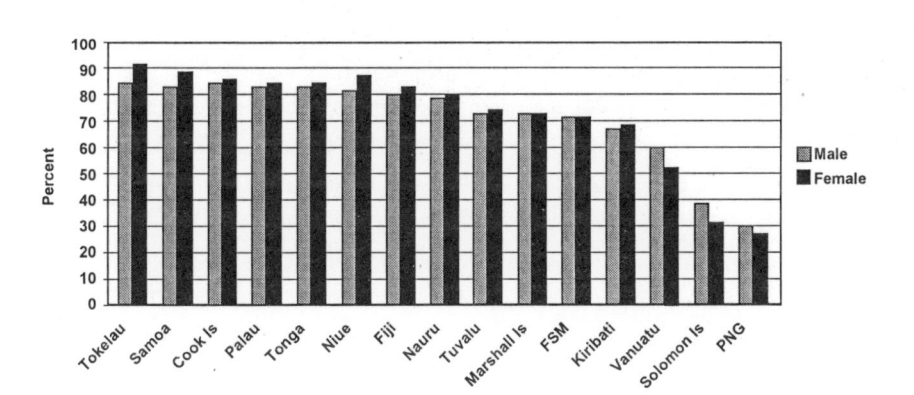

Figure 2. Gross enrolment ratios, by sex, in Pacific island countries

Measuring Participation in Non-Formal Education Programmes

Governments and development organizations recognize that non-formal education programmes are effective and cost-efficient ways to assist people to gain productive skills. Over the past decade, these training courses have expanded rapidly. Still, there are far fewer places available than there are potential students. The difficulty is in quantifying this short-fall in supply, and the gender gap within it, in order for policymakers to better realize the demand for non-formal education.

Non-formal programmes take a variety of forms. Long courses, often of one to three years duration, are run by rural training centers, most sponsored by churches and mostly for young men. Shorter courses are conducted by various organizations, often on a "one-off" basis, sometimes running for a few weeks.

These courses also vary a lot in their content, giving training in a wide range of skills, from basic literacy and numeracy to money management and business skills. The longer courses mostly teach vocational skills, often using formal training methods since many of the instructors are ex-school teachers. Most focus on production skills and give little attention to the business and entrepreneurial skills that small or micro-business operators also need. Some programmes, however, are quite innovative such as those that include community development skills in their curricula and that train people in project design, planning and management. Others address the problems that people and communities face in reconciling traditional values with capitalist business practices, and teach people how to manage special loans, manage businesses, and develop enterprises of different sizes. This difference in duration and content makes measuring participation quite difficult. How does one compare participation in a three-year vocational course with participation in an intermittent community training programme?

There are other indications that there are far too few opportunities for people to participate in these programmes. A 1998 survey in Fiji found that 10,950 applications were received in the year for a total of 4,850 places in eight major non-formal vocational programmes, or twice as many applicants as the places available. But neither number represents the real demand for this training, for many people either do not know of the programmes or decide against applying. Most people hear about these courses by word of mouth, for there is no public listing of the training opportunities available. Sometimes this information hardly comes into the public domain at all because the concerned organizations themselves select the people to train, rather than allow individuals to apply according to their own assessment of their needs.

There has been very little assessment of these programmes, or of formal vocational programmes for that matter. One way to do this is through tracer studies that document the success or failure of graduates of these programmes. This especially needs a gender focus, for in their prior identification of participants, programme organizers often reveal their preconceptions about gender roles, thereby effectively denying individuals their choice and also removing opportunities for these gender stereotypes to change.

Table I shows the number of students enrolled at rural training centers in the three Melanesian countries—Papua New Guinea, Solomon Islands and Vanuatu. This number represents only a small proportion of the number of school-leavers each year.

Table 1

Students at rural training centers in Melanesian countries, 1995

Country	Approximate number of students (in 1-3 year courses)	Approximate number of young people leaving school each year
Papua New Guinea	11,200 (7,700 male; 3,500 female)	45,000
Solomon Islands	1,900 (1,200 male; 700 female)	7,500
Vanuatu	300 (210 male; 90 female)	4,000

Source: UNDP, 1998.

Throughout the region there needs to be a larger and more concerted approach to skills training, and a better match between the courses available and the needs and aspirations of the students. Vocational training is in particularly short supply. There is a strong male bias in the courses available. More opportunities need to be created for women and girls.

THE POLICY VALUE OF BETTER INFORMATION

One recent study concluded that although the need for more training in basic and productive skills is expressed in almost all national development strategies, non-formal education has not yet become a dynamic or proactive force for change in the Pacific (Cole, 1996). Another survey concluded that while many governments say that they are committed to non-formal education they in fact limit it, restrict it to peripheral areas, and give it less status and fewer resources than formal education (Hill, 1986). Specific national policies are needed in regard to non-formal education backed by serious concern and funding. Moreover, the diplomas and other credentials that non-formal education programmes confer should be given greater recognition by government and other formal employers, for graduates of these programme are often locked out of mainstream training and job opportunities (UNDP, 1998).

These problems reflect the low status that is given to vocational education in general, and to non-formal education in particular. Better assessment of participation rates in educational programmes is a critical step towards both improving the policy environment and designing and targeting programmes for the demand that exists. The ad hoc process by which educational programmes are currently designed in the Pacific islands denies many people the opportunities they want, and too many of these people are women.

Works Cited

Cole, R. 1996. *Pacific 2010: Opportunities for Non-formal Education in Melanesia*. Canberra: National Centre for Development Studies, Australian National University.

Hill, H. 1986. Non-formal Education and Development: A Study with Particular Reference to Three Territories of the Pacific. Unpublished PhD thesis. Australian National University.

UNDP, 1998. *Sustaining Livelihoods: Promoting Informal Sector Growth in Pacific Island Countries*. Suva.

UNDP, 1999. *Pacific Island Countries' Human Development Report, 1999: Creating Opportunities*. Suva.

THE DAWN REVIEW OF THE ICPD IMPLEMENTATION IN THE SOUTH:
SUBSTANTIVE AND METHODOLOGICAL ASPECTS OF MONITORING

Josefa Francisco

The Context of the DAWN Review

Since it was organized by women in Nairobi in 1985, the Development Alternatives with Women for the New Era or DAWN has been strongly involved in global debates on development issues. DAWN was active in the series of UN conferences held between 1992 (UNCED) and 1995 (WSSD and FWCW), where it produced a number of platform documents that articulated a Southern feminist perspective on the various conference themes and concerns. DAWN's perception of what these global debates have thus far produced is aptly summed up by our research coordinator on reproductive rights, sexuality and gender justice: "... these exercises have enormously contributed to consensus building across regions as well as between the North and the South. This strength made possible the paradigm shift in the International Conference on Population and Development (ICPD) which was reiterated and expanded in the subsequent UN Conferences, most particularly in the Beijing Platform of Action. In 1998 our conceptions have become legitimized as a new international normative consensus..." (Correa, 1998a).

These global documents were in themselves victories for the global women's movement, victories within a negotiated space that is dominated by states and international donor agencies. We do have feminists and allies working in governments and international agencies, but it is important not to lose sight of the fact that these spheres are distinct and separate from the activist women's movement and that they often present enormous limitations and difficulties for any feminist advocate. Moreover, the discursive space of the UN conferences was and continues to be largely shaped by the demands of and dynamics between governments and international agencies. While the voices and perspective of non-governmental groups have become stronger in this realm, we are still far from having an international mechanism and consensus that is jointly and equally participated in by citizens and states.

What Did We Mean by Monitoring?

Having been participants in the sexual and reproductive health and rights advocacy around the ICPD, DAWN was keen to critically understand how Southern governments and international agencies were implementing their Cairo commitment, and to identify areas that could be improved in terms of policies and services. We believed that a strategic factor in ensuring that Southern women's lives benefited from the ICPD was an enabling environment in which the interaction and dynamics between three important stakeholders—the women's movement (in particular sexual and reproductive health and rights advocates), national governments, and international donor agencies—mattered.

By examining country-level implementation with this analytical lens, our aim was to influence, together with other women's/feminist networks, the substantive debates in the Cairo + 5 UN meeting. As much as possible, we networked with similar monitoring efforts on ICPD implementation being carried out by women's groups and NGOs.

At the regional and national levels, we aimed to support the advocacy and substantive work of activist women's groups and feminists. This was undertaken through either regional consultations convened by DAWN, as was the case in Africa, or tie-ups with regional groups that were, in turn, linked with national groups. In Southeast Asia, the regional link was ARROW and in the Philippines, a DAWN report was shared with Likhaan, the NGO focal point for ICPD + 5, and Womanhealth Philippines.

Because we are rooted in the South, we immediately factored in the diversity and heterogeneity of this broad "South" conception. We needed to be context-specific in our reporting, i.e., in terms of the general attitude of the governments to important elements of the ICPD; the existing state of advocacy of women's groups/networks within civil society; and participation/non-participation of international agencies in country- and region-level dynamics around the ICPD. Secondly, DAWN factored in its view that "the global and national environment(s) do not favor the full implementation of ICPD recommendations" (Correa, 1998a). This assumption is based on the political economy of globalization explored in yet another DAWN research effort (Sen, 1998). Given the ongoing economic crisis that is affecting major regions in the South and East, the trend towards privatization in health sector reform initiatives, as well as the difficulties faced by the Highly Indebted Poor Countries (HIPCs), we suspected that ICPD commitments would be influenced, if not compromised, by lack of funds. We wanted to examine how this was going on everywhere in the South. Finally, we knew at the outset that the ICPD was a "complex" and "contentious" document, hence we expected to find bottlenecks and problem areas in adoption and implementation by states and international agencies, as well as ongoing debates on some issues (e.g., abortion, sexual rights) of particular concern to activist women's groups.

An "Open and Flexible" Qualitative Framework Focused on the Policy Environment

In defining the framework, we began by isolating the elements of the ICPD that "clearly imply a feminist perspective on population related policies" (Correa, 1998a). These include the following sections: "Enabling Environment"; "Sexual and Reproductive Health Policies and Programs and the Exercise of Sexual and Reproductive Rights"; "The Role of NGOs: Governmental and Non-Governmental Relations"; and "Financial Aspects Implied in the Implementation of Reproductive Health Programs". The DAWN research coordinator provided all researchers with a guide delineating the different provisions in the document that were relevant to each of the areas cited above.

Being flexible meant that country/regional researchers and writers, who were feminist activists involved in sexual and reproductive rights advocacy, were free to choose any set of policies that they believed were strategic in the national and/or regional political, economic, and socio-cultural environment. They were also left to decide on what relative importance or value was to be assigned to specific policies.

Clearly, we were not concerned with population and other demographic statistics per se. Rather, these were to be taken on board if and when necessary to support analysis or, put another way, only for meeting the evidentiary requirements of certain assertions. (Statistics on adult literacy, I believe, will have to figure prominently in any monitoring of state compliance with CONFINTEA. Such is in contrast to the negligible value given to population statistics in the DAWN review on ICPD.)

All of the country studies and regional analyses inter-linked three aspects: the pre-Cairo scenario, ICPD recommendations relevant to the country condition, and the post-Cairo scenario (Correa, 1998b). We understood "scenario" to mean not only objective conditions (statistics, policies, programs, and services) but also the state of debates and substantive contestations in the policy arena. We recognized that the complexity of the ICPD was in fact a product of intensive and still unresolved ideological and interpretive conflicts over certain ICPD statements and recommendations. (Again to relate this with the topic on hand, I am sure that in the realm of adult education, one may find also conceptual tensions and conflicting interpretations.)

The Need in Monitoring to Understand the Micro-Macro Link

In our highly globalized environment, monitoring of the implementation of an international agreement is an exercise in micro-macro linking and analysis. After all, international agreements are products of negotiations at the global level involving different states and peoples. In the ICPD, the fact that several international donor agencies, foremost of which is UNFPA, are in the forefront of seeing through its implementation, internationalizes population and development programs and services. There is too the fact that Northern countries and their aid agencies have made it their business to support population activities everywhere in the South. Moreover, Northern-based women's groups and feminist activities have directed much of their activism around the ICPD.

This is not to say that the South—states and women's groups alike—do not have their reasons for supporting the ICPD. However, from the perspective of a political economy of economic globalization and development adopted by DAWN—in which Southern states suffer from mal-development arising from a highly uneven distribution of the world's wealth and power, as well as from a TINA ("there is no alternative") syndrome stirred by a dominant discourse on development—Southern states, poor peoples, and women face multiple barriers in achieving real development. Understanding the nexus of the internal-external or the macro-micro can provide a sharper context for social and political analysis that monitoring of the implementation of international agreements invariably entail.

Below are some pointers on monitoring projects:

BE CLEAR WITH YOUR FOCUS. International agreements are often complex and made up of several parts. As such, they often do not lend themselves to an assessment within a single and comprehensive study. Data requirements will also vary depending on what agreement or recommendation is being monitored. Activists may not have the technical ability or the time, nor even be the best placed persons/group to gather the required data and carry out the appropriate analysis. Having a set of themes or agreements to focus on will make for a stronger position in effective advocacy, as against a "comprehensive" review whose data and analysis are patchy.

DEFINE YOUR OVER-ALL POLITICAL AIM. As activists, we are not in the business of taking the place of governments and international agencies in obtaining the appropriate data for monitoring country trends and status. We conduct monitoring because of the political aim of making governments and international agencies accountable for certain commitments made at the international level. Governments often make several commitments, and we may not have the time, resources or capacities to monitor all of them. We therefore need to isolate the strategic areas that we will include in our monitoring exercise.

INVOLVE ACTIVIST ORGANIZATIONS AND WOMEN WHO HAVE BEEN A PART OF THE ADVOCACY AROUND THE AGREEMENTS IN YOUR MONITORING PROJECTS. Monitoring of implementation is a logical follow-up to our work of pressuring states to make progressive commitments at the international level. Those among us who had been active in the activities leading up to the agreements can provide a historical perspective and make a substantive contribution to the debates surrounding the original conference and subsequent consensus document. At the same time, it is good to have the "veterans" work alongside other groups and individuals who can bring in a fresh perspective and lend their necessary experience to the monitoring project.

Combine the use of qualitative and quantitative data for monitoring specific commitments. There are many commitments we wish to monitor which can be discussed more substantively by way of qualitative data. Quantitative data are definitely impressive but may be no more useful than for providing us with some general context for our analysis of other substantive areas of commitment. It will be useful as well for activist groups to include a discussion of the unavailability of statistics to civil society groups, or of the simple absence of government censuses and surveys. These have a bearing on the broader question of transparency and accountability, not just on government's (in)efficiency.

In conclusion, let me reiterate DAWN's view that monitoring is a political project that should serve the activist interest of feminist networks and people's organizations. Specifically, it is a means by which we can sustain our ongoing policy debate with governments, nationally and internationally, and secure the gains we fought hard to make in the previous conferences.

WORKS CITED

Correa, Sonia. 1998a. DAWN research document on ICPD+5 Review.

_____. 1998b. In DAWN Informs 2/98.

Sen. 1998. In DAWN Informs 2/98.

Appendix

Table No. 1. Dimensions of Empowerment and Expected Changes Brought About by Empowerment Processes

Dimensions of empowerment	Expected changes brought about by empowerment processes facilitated by a development institution.
Personal empowerment	Increase in the ability to: 1.1. formulate and express ideas and opinions 1.2. participate and influence new spaces 1.3. learn, analyse, act 1.4. see that things are possible/overcome fatalism 1.5. organize personal time 1.6. obtain/control resources 1.7. interact outside the home
Close relationships (family/community)	Increased control over personal circumstances: 2.1. income 2.2. fertility 2.3. mobility 2.4. use of time 2.5. possibility of attending meetings, training courses, trips 2.6. personal respect 2.7. self-decision-making
Collective	3.1. negotiation with other organizations, including the state 3.2. ability to generate external resources 3.3. ability to respond collectively to external events 3.4. increased access to material resources (land, capital, loans, technologies, etc.) 3.5. ability to assemble/initiate organization networks

Table No. 2. Cenzontle: Programs and Promoted Activities and Their Link to the Generation of Empowerment Indicators

Expected future impacts	Services offered that are linked to these impacts	Empowerment indicators that can emerge from the promoted activities
Ability to participate politically	1.1. training in conflict resolution	1.1. number of women and/or groups that act at the local level (Diplito, Esteli, Managua) to enable institutions to offer the best quality of basic services, or number of women and/or groups that have maximum population coverage
	1.2. leadership and citizenship training	1.2. a) number of women who actively participate in electoral processes; b) who are candidates; c) who hold public office
	1.3. training in community participation	1.3. same as 1.1
	1.4. training in the "Women and Politics" process	1.4. number of women who participate in the drafting of women agenda

	advocated by Cenzontle, within the framework of the Latin American Network of Women and Politics	
		1.5. number of women who participate in the activities of the women's movement
Security and economic growth	2.1. granting of credit	2.1. a) number of women who receive credit and who return it in due time and manner; b) number of women who raise the credit level in relation to previous years
	2.2. granting of techni-cal assistance to selected groups and entrance to growth and product specialisation processes	2.2. number of selected women who diversify their economic activities after technical assistance
	2.3. training in basic accounting	2.3. number of women who do basic accounting in their businesses and/or in the groups to which they belong
	2.4. training in business	2.4. number of women who improve their income level (income during the present year in relation to income the previous year; annual average converted to dollars)
	2.5. training in basic administration	
Increased levels of self-esteem	3.1. training in self-esteem	3.1. number of women who make decisions about the use of economic resources in their homes
	3.2. training in gender and the sexual division of labour	3.2. number of women who show that in their homes domestic chores are actually distributed among men and women
	3.3. agreements with other institutions in order to educate users on family planning and sex education	3.3. number of women into family planning and sex education
	3.4. training in women's legal rights	3.4. number of women who participate in workshops and training courses promoted by Cenzontle
More efficient organization levels	4.1. organization of women's groups for credit	4.1. a) permanence of the groups; b) collective initiatives to obtain resources or services for the group's benefit
	4.2. organization of groups within the Technical Assistance, Economic Development, and Business Formation programs	4.2. groups who are involved in collective projects relating to economic development
	4.3. organization of multipliers	4.3. women multipliers

SOURCE: 1998-2000 Strategic Plan; 1997 Draft of the Annual Evaluation Report

OUTPUT OF THE GROUP WORK

Group One

LEVELING-OFF CONCEPTUAL UNDERSTANDING OF "GENDER", "ADULT EDUCATION", "MONITORING" AND "EVALUATION"

- gender: sharing/discussion of country experiences on mixed (men and women) and women-only approaches; group consensus that there is a need to create a space for women first—only after can women negotiate, assert and push for women's rights
- group consensus that the social, cultural and political situation of countries provide the context for understanding gender; must not see gender in isolation from such context
- realization of "ideal" society is a million years in the making
- discussion about development as empowering people, especially women, to have more control over their lives and communities; sustainable development assumes that people know more about their needs and how to satisfy them; also, that outside resources only facilitate the capacity of people
- group consensus that adult education prepares learners for a more "humane-centered and values-based/values-driven" society; it must promote values associated with women, such as nurturing and caring, to overcome the destructive values of the mainstream

METHODOLOGY AND PARTICIPATION

- discussion focused on what monitoring and evaluation (M&E) would best reflect the gains of the struggles of grassroots women's groups, organizations, as well as the women's movement; group consensus that only through reflecting the gains and struggles can the women's agenda be brought up to the international/policy level; the shift in gender policy would be the best indicator
- discussion on the tendency to impose mind-sets/concepts from the top, not from the ground; since grassroots women don't "think" or "speak" in terms of concepts, how can we bring to the fore women's views based on actual experiences on the ground, and conceptualize based on these views (e.g., the valorization of "life skills")?
- discussion on negative experiences in M&E, e.g., M&E associated with fear and other negative values in direct contrast to feminist values of non-hierarchy and trust; group consensus on the values-based M&E, i.e., non-threatening, based on trust, non-hierarchical (involving real, not token, participation of women on the ground); M&E must be built into projects
- group consensus that success stories must be a substantial part of M&E; however, mistakes of and dilemmas in projects must not be hidden in M&E, this being the tendency today
- group consensus that current M&E fails to capture the nuances of conscientisation, which is the essence of women and development; there is a need to qualify this concept through the many experiences of grassroots women
- group consensus that the best indicators (not in the strict, statistical sense) are those that reflect the changes in power relations; changes in power relations can be measured best through the stories of women as they relate to the different contexts of home/family, community, state/larger society; current M&E is very weak in this aspect, thus the need to develop it

SPECIFIC ACTION PLANS

1) revision of papers such that M&E becomes the focus of the discussion; revisions must be based on interactions in this workshop, must be sensitive to points raised with respect to the paper presentations as well as in the workshop discussions; lessons with regards to M&E must be emphasized
2) UNESCO to formulate guidelines for M&E from a gender perspective based on the papers presented, which would then be given to the participants
3) participants should follow these guidelines when they return to the field
4) preparation of No. 3 above as inputs to the Rio + 10 conference

Group Two

What we are trying to achieve is an analytical framework in which the monitoring and evaluation data applicable to any education gender issue could be identified. *Vision* informs all aspects of the framework. *Issue* is defined as strictly as possible. Two issues are identified here. There are, of course, many others. As others are identified, many linkages between the frameworks would become obvious. *Data collection* and *data production* relate to the information needed to address the issue identified and how the data is to be gathered. *Necessary action* describes what must be done in sequential order. *Actors/participants* describes who is responsible. The latter three together constitute the *Plan of Action*.

Vision	Issue	Data Collection	Data Production	Necessary Action	Actors/Participants
Political commitment to equal women's education and advancement (through ratification of CEDAW, CONFINTEA, national policies)	HOW THE EDUCATION SYSTEM ADDRESSES THE PROBLEM OF MARGINALISATION OF WOMEN	• sex stereotypes [Q2], in curricula, materials and course structures [Q1] • analyses of formal and informal employment data by sector and by vocation; by gender [Q1] • analysis of leadership data (political, economic, social, traditional) by gender [Q1,Q2] • data on life histories [Q2]	• textual analysis of curricula materials at all levels, formal and non-formal • survey on course entrance opportunities • national consensuses and surveys, and other national data collection machinery • at micro scale, requires project-level data, such as tracer studies on how education has transformed the lives of people.	Political commitment to and resources for data collection ↓ analyses, syntheses, programmatic discussions involving all stakeholders ↓ positive action versus discrimination vs. women	government NGOs private sector ↓ women at different educational levels, across the socio-economic spectrum

Vision	Issue	Data Collection	Data Production	Necessary Action	Actors/Participants
Political commitment to adult education (through ratification of CEDAW, CONFINTEA, national policies) Feminist values: equity, social justice, social action, transformation Individual rights and responsibilities	ACCESS TO ADULT EDUCATION	a) Overall Participation • sex ratio of participants [Q1] • proportion of male/female participants vs. adult pop. [Q1] b) Type of Course (content, fee-paying or not, provider, organiser, time, etc.) [Q1,Q2] → pattern of marginalisation by gender emerges c) Information about marginalised groups [Q1, Q2] d) Information about non-participants [Q1, Q2]	requires national policies & commitments • backed by special questions in censuses or other national machinery for data collection (resources provided by gov't; data collected by gov't, NGOs, private sector) • at micro-scale, requires project level data, e.g., tracer studies that identify conditions and variables that are relevant to the transformation of the lives of people	censuses, surveys (at both macro and micro levels); participatory research ↓ analyses, syntheses, programmatic discussions involving all stakeholders ↓ action to counter policies and actions that restrict women's access to education	government NGOs private sector ↓ Participants in education programmes, especially women

Group Three

PHILOSOPHY: IMPROVING THE QUALITY OF EDUCATION; THIS MAY OR MAY NOT LEAD TO SOCIAL CHANGE

IMPORTANCE OF MONITORING AND EVALUATION (M&E)
- accountability issues for all stakeholders
- helping us to improve on what we do

STATE OF M&E IN ADULT EDUCATION
- dominance of quantitative evaluation in some places
- externally-driven evaluation by donors
- NGOs' tendency to use qualitative data for highlighting only "success" stories; NGOs are not self-critical enough
- there are aspects of adult education that are overlooked in current M&E indicators/efforts, e.g., "reward" or "sense of self-worth" of facilitators
- while M&E should be institutionalized in organisations, NGOs do not always have adequate capacity in M&E
- NGOs can sometimes lose objectivity in evaluating their own projects; there is a need to acquire some "professional" skills
- learners very rarely get feedback from M&E
- current M&Es are focused narrowly on project framework
- gender is rarely factored into project design, or is sometimes "pushed" into the project midway by donors

WHAT DO WE WANT TO SEE IN M&E DESIGNS AND APPROACHES?
- equal focus on methodology and content in M&E
- participation of learners in M&E
- scope of M&E to be expanded to include linkages of project with national/international goals
- a negotiated, not imposed, gender framework should be incorporated in the project design; this framework should be discussed by the NGO-community and donors
- gender can be negotiated within the expanded definition of adult education

CHALLENGES
- in many places, the women's movement is *not* interested in adult education
- diminishing funds for adult education in Southern countries
- not everyone in adult education is gender-sensitive; leadership is strongly male-oriented

METHODOLOGY

In addition to measuring the gender gap:
- *examine factors—social, cultural, economic, institutional—that impinge on women's participation*
- *examine quality of non-formal education*, including teaching materials, trainers/facilitators; at the most basic, content analyse images and messages for their gender content
- *examine "motivation" aspect and change in behaviour and attitude over time*
- gender mainstreaming means integrating gender into other learning concepts, learning objectives, and life skills and conditions; *examine this process of integration*
- *examine participatory process* as this is vital to empowerment, which is one of the goals of adult education
- *institute regular monitoring within the organisation*
- *create an oversight committee or body on mainstreaming gender in adult education*